Comparative Psychology

Human and Animal Behaviour: A Sociobiological
Approach

ARTS & COMMUNICATION
RESOURCE CENTRE

INTRODUCTORY PSYCHOLOGY

This series of titles is aimed at psychology students in sixth forms and further education colleges and at those wishing to obtain an overview of psychology. The books are easy to use, with comprehensive notes written in coherent language; clear flagging of key concepts; relevant and interesting illustrations; well-defined objectives and further reading sections to each chapter; and self-assessment questions at regular intervals throughout the text.

Published

INDIVIDUAL DIFFERENCES
Ann Birch and Sheila Hayward

DEVELOPMENT PSYCHOLOGY
Ann Birch and Tony Malim

COGNITIVE PROCESSES
Tony Malim

SOCIAL PSYCHOLOGY
Tony Malim and Ann Birch

COMPARATIVE PSYCHOLOGY
Tony Malim, Ann Birch and Sheila Hayward

PERSPECTIVES IN PSYCHOLOGY
Tony Malim, Ann Birch and Alison Wadeley

Forthcoming

BIOPSYCHOLOGY
Sheila Hayward
RESEARCH METHODS AND STATISTICS
Tony Malim and Ann Birch

COMPARATIVE PSYCHOLOGY

Human and Animal Behaviour: A Sociobiological Approach

Tony Malim, Ann Birch and Sheila Hayward

MACMILLAN

First published 1996 by
MACMILLAN PRESS LTD
Houndmills, Basingstoke, Hampshire RG21 6XS
and London
Companies and representatives
throughout the world

ISBN 0–333–63918–9

A catalogue record for this book is available
from the British Library.

10 9 8 7 6 5 4 3 2 1
05 04 03 02 01 00 99 98 97 96

Printed in Malaysia

Cartoons by Sally Artz

Series Standing Order (Introductory Psychology)

If you would like to receive future titles in this series as they are published, you can make use of our standing order facility. To place a standing order please contact your bookseller or, in case of difficulty, write to us at the address below with your name and address and the name of the series. Please state with which title you wish to begin your standing order. (If you live outside the United Kingdom we may not have the rights for your area, in which case we will forward your order to the publisher concerned.)

Customer Services Department, Macmillan Distribution Ltd
Houndmills, Basingstoke, Hampshire RG21 6XS, England

Contents

List of Figures and Tables

Figures

Boxes

vii

Preface

This book aims to provide an introduction to the comparative study of human and animal behaviour. It takes as its starting point the evolutionary pressures which have influenced the behaviour of humans and animals. Chapter 1 provides an introduction to the evolution of behaviour from a sociobiological perspective, outlines the main fields of study in this area and includes a commentary on methods of study and the ethical considerations which are involved. Chapter 2 is concerned with the ways in which both instinctive and learned behaviour contribute to the adaptation of animals to their environments. Chapter 3 focuses particularly upon learning, both simple and more complex. In Chapter 4 the focus turns to communication among animals and ends with a discussion of attempts which have been made to teach animals human language. Finally, in Chapter 5 there is discussion of the social organisation of animals. Throughout the book an attempt has been made to use an examination of the behaviour of animals to throw light upon human behaviour. While it is clearly unwise to extrapolate too closely from animal to human behaviour, attention has been drawn to ways in which similar influences apply to both.

As with the rest of the books in this series the intention is to provide a concise framework of comprehensive notes which may be used as a basis for further study. Each chapter begins with objectives to be met, and at the end of each section there are self-assessment questions to help independent students test their understanding of the section. Readers are advised to work carefully though the text, one section at a time, before considering the self-assessment questions following it. After further study or reading the questions may be re-examined.

The focus of the book is mainly those who are involved with GCE A-level and GCSE. It is, however, of more general value to those with an interest in animal behaviour. This may include students on degree courses as well as student nurses and midwives, BTEC students and anyone else encountering psychology for the first time. We have confidence that this book will prove to be stimulating and enjoyable.

Tony Malim
Ann Birch
Sheila Hayward

Acknowledgements

The authors gratefully acknowledge the help and assistance of Stephen Lea of the the Dept of Psychology, Exeter University, for his very helpful and detailed comments both on the outline and later on the draft of this book.

Sally Artz is responsible for the creation of the cartoons which appear at the beginning of each chapter and our thanks are due to her once again.

The authors and publishers are grateful to the following for permission to reproduce an illustration: Figure 3.6 is reprinted with permission from *An Introduction to Animal Behaviour*, 4th edn, by A. Manning and M. S. Dawkins, published by Cambridge University Press.

Introducing the Study of Animal Behaviour

1

At the end of this chapter you should be able to:

1. Provide some reasons why psychologists should be interested in studying animals.
2. Describe what is meant by *continuity* and *discontinuity* as regards the relationship between animals and humans.
3. Identify the main features of Darwin's theory of evolution and say how this relates to continuity.
4. Outline the main features of the process of genetic transmission.
5. Show what is meant by the sociobiological perspective as it relates to comparative psychology and identify some of the objections raised to it.
6. Outline the main features of gene-culture co-evolution of the human species.
7. Show some understanding of methods used in the study of animal behaviour.
8. Show an appreciation of the importance of the observance of ethical standards in the study of animal behaviour.

INTRODUCTION

The authors have been in some difficulty with the title of this book. 'Comparative Psychology' does not really reflect the present thought on animal behaviour, but yet it remains the title of a section of the Psychology A-level syllabus. Accordingly, it is perhaps as well to set out the rationale and perspective from which the book has been approached. It has been sub-titled 'A Sociobiological Approach' advisedly. What this implies is that all behaviour, certainly among animal species, and probably among human animals as well, is driven by an overarching need, that of the individual animal to pass its genes on to succeeding generations. Behaviour which does not contribute to this end will tend to die out, to be replaced by behaviour which does more to ensure that the genes an individual carries are transmitted to offspring.

It is important to stress that this does not imply any motivation on the part of individual animals to maintain their species; indeed, there are instances where the need of individuals to perpetuate their genes has led to species diversification.

At a later point in this chapter we shall discuss the origins of the sociobiological approach to the study of animal behaviour and its implications for human animals. We have refrained from extrapolating to too great an extent from animal to human behaviour, but the reader is invited to draw conclusions, bearing always in mind that there are vast differences between animals and humans – as well as some surprising similarities. Comparative psychology does after all imply comparison!

SECTION I   INTRODUCTION

Why do psychologists study animals anyway? It is possible to suggest several cogent reasons:

- Animal behaviour is interesting for its own sake. This is particularly true for psychologists, as their interests lie in studying behaviour.
- Knowledge gained from the study of animal behaviour can often provide fresh insights into human behaviour.
- There are many contexts in which the lives of animals and of humans interact – in farms, for instance, or in zoos. For example, some zoos no longer keep polar bears in captivity, as studies of their behaviour have shown that they sometimes become mentally disturbed.
- There is also the purely practical point that studying animals is sometimes more convenient. There are two main reasons:

  1. They reproduce more rapidly so that their behaviour can be easily studied across more than one generation.

2. They are more controllable. Experimentation is about the control of variables and where animals are subjects this control is more easily achieved. It needs to be borne in mind that control has an ethical side to it and this will be discussed later in this chapter.

Continuity or Discontinuity

The crucial point concerns the concept of **continuity** between humans and animals. This is a philosophical and religious issue. The question is whether humans and animals are one creation with continuity of development between them or whether humans and animals are separate and unrelated creations. The Book of Genesis puts it like this:

And God made the beast of the earth after his kind, and cattle after their kind and every living thing that creepeth upon the earth after his kind: and God saw that it was good. And God said 'Let us make Man in our own image, after our own likeness.' (Holy Bible: Genesis, ch. 2)

This has been interpreted to mean that there were separate creations for each species of animal and for human beings. That is to say there was **discontinuity** between animals and humans. If discontinuity were accepted, there would be little point in studying animals to find out more about humans.

In 1859 Charles Darwin published *The Origin of Species* which suggested there was an evolutionary link between humans and animals, that they were in fact one creation with different species occupying different places on the evolutionary tree. Not unnaturally this caused a furore among those who regarded the Bible as the literal and inspired word of God but at the same time it opened the way for scientific research to compare the behaviour of animals with that of humans.

The Mechanisms of Genetics and Evolution

1. The mechanism of **genetics** refers to the way in which characteristics are passed on from parents to offspring within a species. Any organism which reproduces sexually possesses a biological inheritance determined by its **genes**. Many vital characteristics are determined in this way and the totality of these characeristics is

known as its **genotype**. An individual's environment (the food it eats, its habitat and the social context in which it lives) interacts with its genes to determine its **phenotype**, the characteristics and behaviour which are evident for all to see. What happens in the case of a simple organism such as a plant may make this clearer. The kind of leaves it has, its flowers and its fruit are determined by its genotype. Its potential maximum and minimum height are also determined genetically, but within these limits the actual height it attains, the amount of fruit or flowers it bears and whether it grows perfectly and without defect may be determined by the environment. This is perhaps an over-simplification because even susceptibility to attack by pests and diseases may be the result of genetic inheritance. It may even have a genetic defect which prevents it using the available soil fertility for growth so that it does not thrive even in the very best of environments.

In human terms, the phenomenon of phenylketonuria (PKU) illustrates this interaction. PKU is a genetic defect which prevents certain individuals from producing an enzyme whose function is to metabolise phenylalinine, which is a common constituent of certain foods, especially dairy products. The build-up of phenylalinine in the bloodstream is toxic, causing mental retardation and eventually death. The toxic effects can be prevented, however, by careful observation of a low protein diet. By itself there are no harmful effects from this genetic defect but sufferers are going to need to observe a very particular diet to avoid problems.

The way in which these genetic principles operate is like this. Every cell in the body contains the same genetic material, produced by the union of two germ cells, one from each parent. This genetic material is carried on **chromosomes**, which come in pairs. In human beings there are 23 pairs of chromosomes. Each chromosome carries two tightly linked strings of DNA molecules, segments of which have been identified as the genes which determine biological features. When cells divide, a process called **mitosis** occurs which duplicates the genetic material in the cell and sends a copy into each new cell. The genes which each of a pair of chromosomes carry are not always identical. Each member of a pair of genes is called an **allele**. These alleles provide alternative blueprints for characteristics. For instance, an individual may possess one allele for blue eyes and one for brown eyes, inherited, one from each parent. In this case the individual would have brown eyes because the gene for brown eyes is **dominant** while that for blue eyes is **recessive.** Blue eyes will not occur unless there is blue-eyed inheritance from both parents, whereas dominant characteristics will be displayed in the phenotype even if only one parent has passed it on. It is important to note that characteristics in an individual are frequently the result of an interaction between several genes. Each gene will determine certain characteristics of form or behaviour. These characteristics do not exist in isolation but in conjunction with each other. For instance, dyslexia is thought to be a genetically based abnormality which adversely affects an individual's ability to read and to write. This abnormality interacts with other genetically determined characteristics which relate to intelligence. A dyslexic person is not lacking in intelligence because of being dyslexic, but the impairment of the ability to read and write may impede the development of intellectual capacities if steps are not taken to mitigate the problem. Dyslexic individuals frequently find themselves placed in classes for 'slow learners'.

When conception occurs, a single germ cell from the father (a sperm cell) merges with a single germ cell from the mother (an ovum) to form a **zygote.** This is the single cell from which the whole organism will develop. The sperm cell and the ovum are exceptional in that they do not have 23 pairs of chromosomes as does every other cell but 23 single unpaired chromosomes which are called **gametes** and are formed by a process called **meiosis.** The pairs of chromosomes first duplicate as in mitosis, then the cells divide twice and produce four cells each with 23 chromosomes. On fertilisation both mother and father contribute one gamete so that there are again 23 pairs of chromosomes in the zygote. Then the zygote divides by mitosis to form all the specialised cells of the body. Another important factor in genetic inheritance is **crossover.** Sections of chromosomes may split off and exchange places before meiosis so that the combination of alleles on the chromosomes is shuffled. This increases the number of possible gametes.

2. The mechanism of **evolution** works like this. Most species produce far more offspring than are needed to maintain numbers. It is inevitable if the balance of numbers is to be maintained, that a high proportion of their young will fail to reach maturity. Those which do succeed in reaching maturity are those best **adapted** to survive in the environment in which they find themselves. Their genes (the innate blueprint which determines their characteristics) are those which

ensure survival. Individuals in a species that carry genes which are less well adapted to survival are less likely to be able to pass on their genes to succeeding generations. When there are changes in the environment individual organisms may need to change too, if they are to survive. The important point is not so much the survival of the individual but the survival of the genes. This point will become important when we come to discuss altruistic behaviour. So, the population of a species as a whole changes over generations to become better adapted to survive. If it is unable to to do this it will eventually face extinction. Any given species, then, is continuously undergoing modifications in its characteristics and its behaviour. An example might make this clearer.

The Peppered Moth has wing colourings which vary from very light to very dark. Whether individuals in that species have light or dark colouring is determined by their genetic make-up (the individual's gene blueprint). This blueprint is passed on into the next generation through the individual reaching maturity, mating and producing offspring. The environmental conditions in which some of these moths live have changed. Industrial development has resulted in heavy smoke deposits on trees and buildings. In these conditions, light-coloured moths stand a much greater chance of being spotted by predators than darker ones. Dark-coloured moths have better camouflage, are less easily spotted and so stand a better chance of passing on their genes (including that for dark colouring) to their offspring. The predominant colouring of the moths changed in this way from light to dark.

So much then for the mechanism of evolution. What are the implications of Darwin's theory for the study of behaviour? Given discontinuity, there was no point in studying any organism other than human beings in order to find out more about human behaviour. They represented, after all, a unique creation. Once Darwin's thesis was accepted the situation changed. It became possible to look not only at the **ontogeny** of a species, that is to say the changes which occur in that species with development and maturation, but also at the **phylogeny**, the point it has reached in evolutionary terms.

Social Darwinism

The introduction of Darwin's ideas on natural selection (Darwin, 1859) provided for some people at the time a seeming justification for a 'laissez-faire' or 'market forces' approach to politics, not unlike that which has been described as 'Thatcherism'. If the development of animal species better adapted to survive is the result of evolution through natural selection then the same set of forces could be seen to be at work within human behaviour. Those individuals within the human species who succeeded best could be seen to have done so in accordance with the natural order of things. Their genes had been responsible for behaviour which was better adapted to their environment and so it was right that they should prosper and pass on this genetic advantage to their heirs. It was not right to try to 'buck the market' by introducing artificial ideas of social justice or reform. Herbert Spencer in his treatise entitled *Social Statics* (1851) put it like this:

> Inconvenience, suffering and death are the penalties attached by nature to ignorance, as well as to incompetence . . . If to be ignorant were as safe as to be wise, no one would become wise. (Spencer, 1851)

Similarly, in 1884 Spencer used Darwinism to defend competitive individualism. So far as Spencer was concerned there were close parallels between economic competition and natural selection. Social evolution could take place most easily in a condition of laissez-faire. Social reform should be limited to charitable benevolence. There was no room for state intervention. Spencer replied to criticisms of him made by T. H. Huxley in these terms:

> Because I hold that the struggle for existence and the survival of the fittest should be allowed to go on in society, subject to those restraints which are involved by preventing each man from interfering with the sphere of action of another, and should not be mitigated by governmental agency, he, along with many others, ran away with the notion that they should not be mitigated at all. I regard proper benevolence as adequate to achieve all those mitigations that are proper and needful. (Spencer, 1884)

However, to liberals of the time Darwinism came to mean something quite different. Patrick Geddes, a zoologist from Edinburgh, attacked Spencer's individualism. A political economy based upon calculations of self-interest symbolised the dissolution of the moral and social ties of contemporary industrial society:

Even on the most sternly biological grounds, so far from a scientific basis for economic deduction being furnished by this 'iron law of competition' . . . (Darwinism) is the accurate converse of this – the golden rule of sympathy and synergy. (Geddes, 1885, p. 36)

Social organisation was seen as being in the forefront of evolutionary development. Moral and ethical behaviour were closely linked to this. Keir Hardie used Darwin to argue for socialism:

Darwin stated emphatically that 'those communities which included the greatest number of the most *sympathetic* members would flourish best' and in so stating he conceded the whole case for which Socialism is contending. It is sympathetic association and not individualistic competition which makes for progress and the improvement of the race. (Keir Hardie, 1907, p. 92)

Darwin's theories, then, were used not only to support individualism but also collective evolution and social reform. But, of course, these attacks are based on the premise that what matters is the good of the species. Evolution is concerned, as we have seen, not with the survival of the species but of the genes. There is also the implication made that fitter is somehow better. This is by no means necessarily the case. The fact that an individual is better adapted to survive in the environment he or she finds himself or herself in. (i.e. fitter) implies no evaluation of better or worse. Besides, the analogy which Spencer and others make between evolution in Darwinian terms (the success of an individual in passing on his or her genes) and social success in terms of increased prosperity has not been proven in any scientific way. The most prosperous (in economic terms) are not necessarily the 'fittest'.

For our purpose, the assumption is made that Darwin was right and that there does exist an evolutionary link between animals and humans. Even so, there still need to be cogent reasons for studying the behaviour of animals rather than simply concentrating upon the study of *human* behaviour. These have already been discussed (p. 2) and there is no need to repeat them here.

Comparative Psychology as an Applied Science

It is often expected that scientific study will have practical applied spin-offs. Here are some of them which relate to comparative psychology:

1. We are not alone on this planet. We share it with many species of animals with which we interact. On farms, animals are managed to serve our own purposes, to produce wool, dairy products and meat, for instance. At home, many of us have pets and again it is not hard to see that an understanding of animal behaviour may contribute not only to our own but to the animals' comfort, health and well-being. In zoos and wild-life parks as well as in the wild, humans have an interest in conserving the habitats of animals and making sure they are successful, particularly that they breed and reproduce. If we understand their normal mating behaviour in the wild, it will be easier to provide the right conditions for them to reproduce in the somewhat artificial conditions of the zoo or the wild-life park. In the case of some endangered species this may be the only way in which the species can survive.

2. By the study of animals, experimental and observational methods may be developed which may then be used in the study of humans. To take a specific example, Kaye and Brazelton (1971) did a detailed study of what went on in feeding sessions between a human mother and her baby. In particular, they studied the relationship between the jiggling a mother does with her baby and the baby's sucking. It appears that jiggling actually lengthens the pauses between bursts of sucking which occurred when the jiggling stopped. The method adopted was not unlike the close, detailed study of animal behaviour which has been termed **ethology.** Kaye and Brazelton's study could be said to fall into the category of **human ethology**, the close observation and study of human behaviour in the natural environment.

3. Besides the *methods* of animal ethology it has been possible sometimes to translate some of the *concepts* also from animal to human study. For instance, the concept of **imprinting** was studied by Lorenz (1958) among others (it is described in greater detail in Chapter 2, Section II) in relation to young birds. This might be related to the

concept of **attachment** explored by Bowlby (1969) with human children.

4. Books such as *Manwatching* by Desmond Morris (1978) have attempted to extrapolate from animal to human study. In this case the non-verbal behaviour of humans is related to animal behaviour. However, it is open to question whether this extrapolation is legitimate.

Evolution and the notion of continuous phylogenetic development is therefore central to this book.

Altruism and Selfishness

The issue of **altruistic** or **selfish** behaviour provides a good illustration of the approach we have taken. Wilson (1975) provides the following definition of altruistic behaviour:

> Blood relatives bestow altruistic favours upon one another in a way that increases the average genetic fitness of the members of the network as a whole, even when this behavior reduces the individual fitnesses of certain members of the group. The members may live together or be scattered throughout the population. The essential condition is that they jointly behave in a way that benefits the group as a whole, while remaining in relatively close contact with the remainder of the population. This enhancement of kin-network welfare in the midst of a population is called **kin selection** . . . When a person (or animal) increases the fitness of another at the expense of his own fitness, he can be said to have performed an act of **altruism**. (Wilson, 1975, p. 117)

What appears on the surface to be social behaviour aimed at promoting the good of the species, sometimes at the expense of individual members of it, is in fact behaviour which promotes the 'fitness' of the genes which members of the group share. For instance, within a hive of honey-bees a large part of the population is related to the queen – daughters, who share 50 per cent of her genes. It makes evolutionary sense, therefore, for workers to be prepared to sacrifice themselves for the queen. They are sterile and so will leave no offspring to inherit their genes. The queen will pass on the workers' as well as her own genes. The concept of **kin selection** to explain altruistic behaviour originated with Darwin's *Origin of the Species.* He found it hard to reconcile evolutionary theory with the behaviour he observed in colonies of social insects.

Wilson identifies three levels of behaviour in this context: altruism, selfishness and spite:

1. *Altruism* (self-sacrifice for the fitness of another) cannot really be said to be altruistic *genetically,* though in the conventional sense it is. If individuals sacrifice themselves for their offspring, the offspring may have their reproductive life ahead of them, while that of the parent may well be over (or, at the least, shorter than theirs). Ensuring the survival of 50 per cent of one's genes is preferable to none of them being passed on.
2. *Selfishness* involves individuals in raising their own 'fitness' at the expense of others'. While this is not laudable, it is at least understandable. However, if the others happen to be two brothers it may, in evolutionary terms, prove to be profitable. A brother will have 50 per cent of the same genes. Two brothers may be capable of passing on as many of an individual's genes as that individual is.
3. *Spite* is demonstrated when individuals lower the 'fitness' of unrelated competitors with no compensating benefit to their own 'fitness'. This too may evolve if the benefits (in terms of 'fitness') for close relatives (brothers or sisters, perhaps) compensate.

In these discussions the term 'fitness' has been used in the way in which Wilson uses it, that is, in terms of genes which are better adapted to survive. Hamilton (1964, 1970, 1971a and b, 1972) has developed the concept of **inclusive fitness.** This amounts to the sum of an individual's own fitness plus the effects of his/her behaviour on the fitness of all his/her relatives. In Hamilton's model a coefficient of relationship r represents the fraction of an individual's genes held through common descent by two individuals. Accordingly, an individual and his/her brother have $r = 1/2$ in common, first cousins $r = 1/8$, an uncle $r = 1/4$ and so on. For altruistic, selfish or spiteful behaviour to evolve the loss of an individual's fitness must be more than compensated for by gains in fitness made by relatives. So, if first cousins only benefited by apparently altruistic behaviour, k (Hamilton's symbol for the ratio of gain in fitness by the relatives to loss of fitness by the individual) would need to be greater than 8. That is to say, there would need to be eight times the benefit to the relatives (or benefit to eight relatives). Where the altruistic behaviour has an effect upon combinations of relatives the number of relatives of each kind are taken into account, together with their coefficients of relationship.

Hamilton deals with selfish behaviour and spiteful behaviour in a similar way. Where an animal acts selfishly this usually results in a gain by that animal in fitness. But this may not be the case if the selfish animal shares too many genes with those animals which lose by the selfish behaviour. Spiteful behaviour, too, needs to result in an *overall* gain for the genes of the spiteful individual.

Reciprocal Altruism

Trivers (1971) extends these ideas further with what he terms **reciprocal altruism.** The example he uses is that of 'Good Samaritan' behaviour in humans. A man dives in to save another from drowning. The drowning man has a 50:50 chance of dying. The chances of the rescuer dying in the attempt are perhaps one in twenty. If at some future date the roles are reversed and the rescuer becomes the rescued, both will have benefited. Each will have traded a 1:2 chance of dying with a 1:10 chance. Where a population at large engages upon such reciprocally altruistic behaviour, the individuals in that population will have enhanced their personal genetic fitness. There are problems with this argument, though. What if the rescued man does not bother to reciprocate? But if cheating tarnishes a person's good name, the momentary advantage gained by cheating on a moral obligation will be outweighed by the later adverse effects on life and reproduction chances.

But while human behaviour is full of examples of altruistic behaviour, reciprocal altruism is rare in the behaviour of animals. However, Wilkinson (1984) describes a remarkable example of reciprocal altruism among vampire bats (*Desmodus rotundus*). A bat needs to find food regularly, making an incision in the victim's skin with its sharp teeth and sucking its blood; if it fails on three successive nights to find food it may die from starvation. But a bat that has not found food will often be fed by another bat regurgitating its blood meal to it. Bats feed their kin in this way but they also feed unrelated animals, especially those which are starving. The criteria for affording such help are the following:

1. They are sensitive to whether a bat is starving or well fed and can assist a starving animal at a cost to itself which is not too high. A starving bat loses weight at a greater rate than a well-fed one. Consequently, the transfer of sustenance from a well-fed donor to a starving recipient gives the recipient more time than the donor loses.
2. Bats associate with particular other individuals over a long period of time and so remember benefits given them.
3. Bats may find themselves short of food at any time so that altruism acts as a kind of insurance policy.
4. Those who donate food will be more favourably placed than others to receive when times are hard. Altruism has a background of selfishness to it.

Some Other Examples of Altruistic Behaviour

In troops of baboons *(Papio ursinus)* dominant males position themselves in exposed locations to watch while others forage. When predators approach the watchers bark to warn the foraging troop and even threateningly approach the intruders (Hall, 1960).

Meerkats take turns to go up to a high look-out point to keep watch for predators (exposing themselves to danger) while other members of the group feed (Macdonald, 1986).

Birds engage in distraction displays to attract the attention of an enemy away from eggs or young. The female nighthawk *(Chordeiles minor)* will fly conspicuously at low level away from it when an intruder approaches her nest, finally settling on the ground in front of the intruder, wings drooping and outstretched (Gramza, 1967) as though she were injured. Alarm calls (described in Chapter 4) attract the attention of an enemy away from other members of the species and towards the caller.

Clearly if kin selection is to operate, then there has to be some means whereby the animals can distinguish kin from non-kin. Holmes and Sherman (1982) studied Belding's ground squirrels *(Spermophilus beldingi)*. In some cases there were females which had been fertilised by more than one male, so that in one litter of young there may well be siblings and half-siblings. In spite of having been born from the same mother and grown up in the same burrow full siblings were less aggressive to each other than they were to half-siblings. The researchers transferred baby squirrels to new litters when they were very young and found that they were less aggressive towards their foster siblings than to strangers but also less aggressive towards their full genetic siblings from their original litters. Not only does familiarity play a part, but there seems also to be a way in which they can recognise their full siblings even when they have not been brought up with them.

Inclusive fitness is about success in leaving offspring, and this may include individuals aiding the offspring of relatives who may be more rewarding reproductively than they can be themselves.

Self-assessment Questions

1. List some reasons why a psychologist might be interested in studying the behaviour of animals.
2. What is meant by *continuity* and *discontinuity*?
3. Describe the mechanisms of genetic inheritance and of genetic evolution.
4. What are some of the practical applications of the results of animal study?
5. How does evolutionary theory explain apparently altruistic behaviour?

SECTION II   FIELDS OF STUDY

Ethology

Ethology is essentially the study of behaviour in the natural environment. Within the field of ethology there has been development not only in the ways in which behaviour is studied but also in what behaviour is studied. There are broadly three areas within ethology:

1. Crook (1970) applied the label **comparative ethologists** to those who studied behaviour in the same way as they studied any other animal characteristics. Differences not only in physical characteristics but also in behaviour may be related to differences in their **ecology**, that is to say, the environments in which they live, the sources of their food and the predators which they have to avoid.

2. Crook also described the study of animal society as **social ethology**. Social ethologists attempt to understand individual animal behaviour

in relation to the social environment in which they live. This new approach by social ethologists, particularly Wilson (1975) and Dawkins (1976), has became known as **sociobiology** and has been seen as the kind of scientific revolution described by Kuhn (1962). Kuhn explains that when a previously held set of assumptions about a subject, its **paradigm**, is challenged so strongly by new evidence that it has to be abandoned a new paradigm takes its place. This kind of revolution occurred in physics, for instance, with Einstein's theory of relativity. In sociobiology animal societies could be treated as biological entities and understood in terms of evolution and natural selection. In terms of method, the question to ask of any behaviour studied is this: 'Will the gene survive which produces that behaviour in an organism living in a particular environment, more especially, a particular social environment?'

3. In addition there are **behavioural ecologists** interested in the way in which the behaviour of an animal interacts with the environment in which it exists. For instance, the establishment of territories by animals is one way in which they can give themselves exclusive access to resources. Territoriality is discussed more fully later in this book (Chapter 5).

Sociobiology

The introduction of sociobiology, providing as it did a basis for the study of the genetic and evolutionary origins of behaviour, not only of animals but also of the human species, was seen by some academics as reactionary. A group calling themselves Science for the People campaigned vigorously against the new study of sociobiology on the grounds that any attempt to provide a biological basis for social behaviour would lead to Social Darwinism. Human applications of sociobiology were to be condemned because of the political dangers posed by such thinking:

> These theories provided an important basis for the enactment of sterilization laws and restrictive immigration laws in the United States between 1910 and 1930 and also for the eugenics policies which led to the establishment of gas chambers in Nazi Germany.
> (Jonathan Beckwith and 14 co-signers of a letter in *New York Review of Books*, 13 November 1975)

This was clearly an extreme reaction but the reasoning behind these condemnations of sociobiology is flawed. Scientific discovery should not be judged for its possible political consequences. What matters is truth. Knowledge provides a better basis than ignorance for combating reactionary attitudes. The more that becomes known about the relationship between biological mechanisms and behaviour the more possible it becomes to deal with abnormal human behaviour. At the same time people cannot absolve themselves entirely from the responsibility that accompanies discovery of the truth. Is it possible, for instance, for those scientists who invented the atomic bomb to absolve themselves entirely from responsibility for its use on Hiroshima and Nagasaki?

A further group of individuals maintained that there was an incoherence in the idea of sociobiology. The natural sciences had a fundamentally different subject-matter and intent from that of the social sciences or humanities. What is unique, most richly structured and most interesting about human existence was permanently beyond biological investigation. Because human beings had free will they were able to reflect upon the consequences of their actions and they were able to create cultures which diverged. There was enormous variation in culture from one society to another which put it beyond the scope of the traditional reductionist biological analysis. These were much more valid criticisms. Free will, cultural diversity and consciousness were the stuff of what being human was about. The challenge faced was to incorporate mind and culture into evolutionary theory.

At this point, it might be useful to identify clearly what is meant here by **culture**. It can be said to be an amalgam of all those behaviours which result not from genetic programming but from interaction with the environment. In human terms, the way in which we live, the kind of houses we build, the sort of work we do and the way in which we treat each other are a part of our culture. That we use knives, forks and spoons to eat our food, while Indians use a hand, is a cultural difference between us. That we walk upright on two legs, while animals mostly go on four, represents a genetic difference between humans and most species of animal.

Gene-Culture Co-Evolution

The result of this challenge has been a continuing pursuit of the ways in which genetic evolution has come together with culture to create the people we are. In their book *Promethean Fire*, Lumsden and Wilson (1983) have outlined some of the ways in which this **gene-culture co-evolution** works. The human species (*Homo sapiens*) has its behaviour determined neither entirely by its genetic makeup, nor entirely as a result of the culture in which individuals live.

Lumsden and Wilson have illustrated this by imagining species of intelligent creatures which they have christened *eidylons* or *xenidrins*. The former, while brilliant and formidable, have their entire thought and behaviour pre-programmed into their genetic makeup. The latter, equally brilliant and formidable, have no constraints at all on their thought and behaviour placed upon them by their genes.

Among *eidylons*, while their behaviour reflects the circumstances in which they find themselves and they react to what goes on around them, the way in which they react has been genetically predetermined. A festival inspires the singing of a ritual hymn but every last note and inflection has been fixed. An accident occurs and those who witness respond with appropriate expressions of shock and grief. But these are entirely invariant. One appropriate response has been pre-programmed into them to every stimulus they might encounter. There are no alternative or optional ways of responding. Even the ways in which they pass their culture on to succeeding generations has been pre-ordained. The young are genetically programmed to hear and receive just one appropriate response.

Xenidrins, on the other hand, have entirely free will. In any set of circumstances any response is possible so that their minds and their behaviour are entirely the products of the accidents of their history, where they live, what they have to eat and what other species of flora and fauna they encounter. This xenidrin world is that which has frequently been postulated by philosophers such as John Locke in the eighteenth century who believed the human mind to be a *tabula rasa*, a blank slate upon which each person's history writes to determine how he/she will behave and respond.

The way in which humans have developed and evolved is different from either of these hypothetical species. If humans had been *eidylons* there would have been no development except as a result of genetic evolution. Differences among individuals in behaviour arising from gene structure or mutations result in differential adaptation to the environment and differential survival and reproductive rates. Where the genetic structure was better adapted, individuals would be more successful in passing on their genes. Humans are faced with continual choices to make as the environment in which they exist changes and, unlike the *eidylons*, they have a degree of free will in making these choices. If this were not the case, if their behaviour were entirely pre-determined genetically, responses to the changing environment would have been too slow to account for the massive advances which have taken the species *Homo sapiens* rapidly so far ahead of other primates.

If on the other hand humans had been *xenidrins*, whose behaviour was entirely governed by free will, it is hard to see how their genetic makeup would have remained unaffected by the choices made. It is inevitable that some choices made will result in greater success in adapting to the environment and consequently greater reproductive ability. The genes which encouraged those choices become more widely spread in the population. New genetic mutations and recombinations will arise to predispose individuals to make these better-adapted choices. The *tabula rasa*, then, is not such a blank sheet as it was.

Evidence from less developed societies than our own suggests that the assumption that children do in general enjoy a well-ordered social world is false. Their behaviour is not governed wholly, or even for the most part, by instructions from adults, and they are left to fend for themselves even more than in advanced societies. But in spite of this, they become socialised into their own group. Their speech, the skills they need in daily life, their facial expressions, their understanding of the lore and ritual of the tribe and other patterns of behaviour become well developed. It seems evident that this could not occur from free will alone but that there must in addition be a set of genetically determined rules and principles which enable them to learn their world speedily. The suggestion is that those who possess a set of innate clues to help them to master the world into which they are born are likely to adapt to it more quickly and more successfully than they would if they were just endowed with problem-solving mechanisms of a very general kind. Those who are most successful in their adaptation leave more of their genes to succeeding generations.

The conclusions reached in *Promethean Fire* have been summarised by Lumsden and Wilson as follows:

- All domains of human life, including ethics, have a physical basis in the brain and are part of biology; none is exempt from analysis in the mode of the natural sciences.
- Mental development is more finely structured than has been generally appreciated in the past; most or all forms of perception and thinking are biased by processes in the brain that are genetically programmed.
- The structure in mental development appears to have originated over many generations through a specialized form of evolution (gene-culture co-evolution) in which genes and culture change together.
- The biases in mental development are only biases; the influence of the genes, even when very strong does not destroy free will. In fact the opposite is the case; by acting on culture through the epigenetic rules, the genes create and sustain the capacity for conscious choice and decision.
- The predispositions originate from an interaction of particular sets of genes and the environment; they can be altered in a precise manner if the appropriate information about them is available.
- Ethical precepts are based on the predispositions, and they too can be altered in a precise manner.
- One result of a strong human science might be the creation of a sophisticated form of social engineering, one that touches the deepest levels of human motivation and moral reasoning.

(Lumsden and Wilson, 1983, pp. 181–2)

Self-Assessment Questions

1. What approaches to the study of animal behaviour did Crook outline?
2. What was the basis for the controversies which surrounded the introduction of sociobiology as a new field of study, integrating the natural and the social sciences? To what extent were the criticisms made of it justified?
3. What is meant by gene-culture co-evolution? What impact did Lumsden and Wilson suggest it had on the development of the human species?

SECTION III   METHODS OF STUDY OF ANIMAL BEHAVIOUR

Ethological Methods

Ethology refers to the study of animals. This may be pure observation free from any manipulation of the environment or it may be experimental, that is to say it may involve some deliberate manipulation of variables in order to be able to observe the results of this manipulation. In Chapter 4, for instance, the observations made by von Frisch (1967) of honey-bees are described. He suggested that the elaborate 'dances' they perform indicate to other members of the hive where the food is to be found. This was the result of close and careful observation *without* manipulation of the environment. Later, Michelsen (1989) constructed a brass model which could be inserted into the hive and made to perform the dance. This amounted to an experimental manipulation of the bees' environment so that the results of this manipulation could be observed.

Laboratory Study of Animals

The behaviour of animals can be studied either in their natural environments or in laboratories. Laboratories enable scientists to exercise greater control over participants. Experimentation is easier with this kind of control. An experimenter can manipulate one or more of the variables in the study in order to observe and to measure the effect of this manipulation on other variables. Perhaps an illustration will make the distinction clearer.

Marler and Tamura (1964) investigated the way in which the song of the white-crowned sparrow, a native of the Pacific coast of America, was affected by early experiences. Different groups of birds were subjected to different early experiences with the object of exploring the contributions made by instinct, on the one hand, and environmental circumstances, on the other, to the way in which their characteristic song developed.

Group A were isolated from other members of their species and never allowed to hear the mature adult song.
Group B were similarly isolated but exposed to the song of other species when juvenile.

Group C were exposed to the song of adults of their species as juveniles.

Group A and Group B ended up singing a song that was recognisably that of their species but simpler and without the regional 'dialects', while Group C when they began to sing did so with a recognisable local dialect. It was noticed that this happened where they were exposed to tape recordings of adult song before they were three months old but not when the exposure was later (say, beyond four months).

In later experiments (somewhat dubious ethically), Konishi (1965) deafened groups of birds by removing the cochlea from the inner ear at various stages in their development. Those who were deafened as juveniles produced only disconnected notes with no phrasing, which was not recognisable as the song of the white-crowned sparrow. This was true even when the birds who were deafened had been exposed to adult song but had not themselves begun to sing. However, once they had begun to sing, deafening left their song unchanged.

The above studies were laboratory experiments where variables were deliberately manipulated to examine the results of this manipulation. The advantage of experimentation of this kind over observation is that besides the closer control of variables it was possible to identify cause. Konishi was able identify feedback (or the lack of it) as determining whether or not the characteristic birdsong of the white-crowned sparrow developed. Contrast this with some of the accounts in Lorenz's (1952) *King Solomon's Ring* which are of observations of natural behaviour.

Laboratory Studies of Conditioning

The above studies, whether in the laboratory or in the natural environment, and whether observational or experimental, are primarily concerned with learning more about animals. Work done by Pavlov at first on classical conditioning, and later by Thorndike and Skinner on instrumental and operant conditioning is less concerned with animal behaviour, and more with the notion of learning and conditioning as a psychological phenomenon. The use of animals was convenient to this end. In the studies of both classical conditioning and operant conditioning the laboratory environment of the animals was totally controlled. Conclusions drawn are about the nature of learning and conditioning and were intended to be applicable to any species, though more recent studies quoted have highlighted the importance of **species-specific** characteristics (that is, those characteristics which are peculiar to a particular species). Differences in such characteristics are reflected in different conditioned behaviour. A full account of these and other studies of learning is in Chapter 3.

Physiological Study of Animals

A further approach to the behaviour of animals is through a study of their physiology. This might include study of the hormonal changes which occur in relation to motivation or perhaps the role which the hypothalamus (a structure in the lower brain) plays in the control of feeding. Chapter 2 includes some reference to physiological studies.

Conclusion

To sum up, then, methods used in the investigation of animal behaviour have included the following:

- The study of animals in their natural environment in order to find out more about animals. This may be observational or else may include some experimentation.
- Laboratory study in carefully controlled environments with the same object.
- Laboratory study using animals with the purpose of investigating psychological phenomena which are as much applicable to humans as to animals. This may be because animals are more convenient to study than are human participants for some of the reasons outlined earlier in this chapter.
- Physiological study of animals.

Self-Assessment Questions

1. What are some of the advantages and disadvantages of studying animals in their natural environment?
2. List two reasons for the laboratory study of animals.

SECTION IV   SOME ETHICAL CONSIDERATIONS

There is now strong and very vocal opposition to any study of animals which could be regarded as invasive. This has even involved violent attacks upon laboratories engaged in animal research and upon academics responsible for these laboratories. However, any experimentation on animals in the United Kingdom is governed by the Animals (Scientific Procedures) Act 1986 and is fairly closely controlled. In addition, guidelines have been issued by the Experimental Psychology Society for those planning research using animals. This section will set out some of the practical and ethical considerations in working with animals, will attempt to justify using animals in psychological research and will consider alternatives to animal experimentation.

Practical Points to be Borne in Mind

1. Humans are qualitatively different from any animal species. Any comparisons made are therefore bound to be imperfect.
2. Those who do not accept *continuity* (as discussed earlier on p. 3) will find no basis at all for studying animals to advance understanding of the human condition. These will include people whose religious convictions lead them to accept the literal truth of the Bible (and in particular the Book of Genesis with its account of creation.)
3. Koestler (1970) has argued that to transfer findings from rats to humans was to commit the sin of **ratomorphism**.
4. There is a danger that researchers may be unable to adopt an objective view of their animal participants, attributing to them human qualities for which there is no real evidence. This is **anthropomorphism.**
5. Animal rights campaigners may well draw on cases where extrapolation of findings about drugs from one species to another has been inappropriate. The implication of this is that if the physiological reactions to the same chemical differ so much between species how can we be confident in transferring findings about behaviour from one species to another?
6. The great strength of experimentation is the degree of control which can be exercised and it is this which gives it its precision. However, there is often a lack of **ecological validity** in

such studies; in other words, they lack reality. Natural or field experimentation, while it has greater realism, loses some of its control and precision.

Ethical Considerations

Besides the practical problems mentioned above, ethical considerations need to be borne in mind. The Experimental Psychology Society has produced some guidelines for those planning experiments using animals:

- Researchers have an obligation to avoid discomfort to all living animals.
- They are also obliged to know the law as it relates to animal research and to acquire the necessary Home Office certification. Proposed projects must be of the highest quality as well as being justifiable on practical grounds. Licences are not lightly granted and proposed researchers have to be suitably qualified people.
- Researchers are required to be thoroughly conversant with the needs of the species they are dealing with and to be as economical as possible in the numbers of animals employed.

The British Psychological Society also publishes a code of conduct for professional psychologists which includes some guidelines on animal welfare and the use of animals in research (1985). They include the following:

- Researchers must keep within the law.
- Consideration must be given as to whether the knowledge to be gained from the study justifies the procedures used. Alternatives to the use of animals should also be considered.
- Choice of appropriate subjects for research should take into account the fact that some species suffer more than others from confinement or research procedures. Animals' special needs should be met and their natural history considered.
- The smallest possible number of animals should be used.
- Apart from serious attempts at conservation, researchers should avoid using endangered species.
- Animals should be obtained from reputable suppliers and records kept of their provenance and their history within the laboratory.

It is up to researchers to confirm that where animals have been trapped in the wild this has been done humanely.

- The social behaviour of a species should be taken into account when animals are caged.
- When fieldwork is carried out animals should be disturbed as little as possible.
- Pain and injury should not be allowed to occur in the laboratory. Studies into aggression or predation should, if at all possible, be carried out via field studies, or if it is necessary to stage encounters between animals, models or animals behind glass should be used.
- Animals' normal eating and drinking habits should be taken into account as well as their metabolic requirements, if researchers are arranging schedules of deprivation. Care needs to be taken to consider differences between species.
- Any procedure which causes pain or distress to an animal is illegal in the UK without a Home Office licence and the necessary certificates. Researchers should first make certain that there is no alternative way of conducting the experiment. Pain and distress caused must be kept to the minimum and must be justified by the scientific contribution which the research makes.
- A Home Office licence and the relevant certificate is necessary before any surgical or pharmacological procedure is carried out. This must be carried out by experienced staff.
- Where anaesthesia is used care must be taken that animals receive adequate post-operative care, suitable nursing and local anaesthetic where this is appropriate so as to avoid unnecessary suffering. If an animal is found to be suffering severe and enduring pain it should be killed. This is also a legal requirement in the UK.
- Where a researcher has any doubt regarding the condition of an animal a second opinion must be sought from someone not involved in the experiments concerned, preferably someone with veterinary qualifications.
- If further advice is required researchers should contact the advisory committees of relevant professional bodies. (British Psychological Society, 1985)

The proportion of psychological research which involves animals is quite small. Coile and Miller (1984) reviewed articles published by the American Psychological Association in the previous five years and reported that out of 608 articles examined only 7 per cent reported research primarily on animals, with 93 per cent studying humans. Miller has stated that there is far more evidence of abuse of animals as pets or as farm stock than there is in research. Gray (1987), writing in reponse to attacks by the British Union for the Abolition of Vivisection (BUAV), makes the following points:

1. Because psychology lacks the clout of the medical establishment it is regarded as a soft target by BUAV. Selective quotation from research papers can make research look pointless.
2. Aims, methods and findings from animal research are not always easy to understand for the lay person. Liberationist literature often presents a distorted view but one which is more easily accessible to lay people.
3. Animals are very widely used by humans, as pets, on farms or for leisure activity (riding, for instance). To single out animal research for condemnation is as illogical as it is unjust. It would be just as logical for the BUAV to seek to ban all use of animals by humans, which would be unrealistic and politically unpopular.
4. The way in which anti-vivisectionists publicise their point of view is emotive. The images they present are by no means representative of animal research. The impression is often given that researchers take gratuitous pleasure in inflicting pain on animals.
5. There exists a structure of committees which decides whether public funds should be used for research. Because of fierce competition for funds, projects have to be well designed, potentially very useful and in line with Home Office rulings.

Bateson (1986) has suggested that a start might be made to resolve the question of animal research by appointing a committee of animal welfare representatives, researchers and disinterested parties to confront three issues:

1. The degree of certainty that there will be medical benefit.
2. The quality of the research.
3. The degree of animal suffering involved.

Alternatives to Animal Experimentation

How can research findings of comparable quality be obtained without using animals in tightly controlled animal experimentation? There seem to be three possible solutions:

1. To concentrate more on methods which involve studying the animals in their natural habitats rather than in laboratories.
2. Alternatives to animal experimentation used in medical research include tissue research and *in vitro* techniques. However, these do not seem to be as applicable to research into animal behaviour.
3. There may be scope for computer simulation, for instance in the field of cognition, but the scope is limited.

In relation also to field experiments in animal behaviour, Cuthill (1991) has reviewed over 100 articles published in *Animal Behaviour* from 1986 to 1990 and identified four sources of ethical problems:

1. Issues of welfare and suffering.
2. Conservation issues.
3. The taking of life *per se*.
4. Issues that arise when human rights are extrapolated to other species.

Dawkins (1990) notes that morally questionable experiments that might be acceptable if the goal is the alleviation of human suffering may not be acceptable if the goal is the satisfaction of intellectual curiosity. She has suggested that some objective basis is needed for deciding when an animal is suffering. Suffering includes a range of unpleasant states (e.g. fear, pain, etc.) that appear to have evolved to avoid danger or to restore physiological defects resulting from the natural environment. Suffering can be said to occur when otherwise healthy animals are prepared to pay a price to attain or to escape from a particular situation. Withholding conditions or commodities for which animals show 'inelastic demand' (i.e. for which they will continue to work despite increasing costs) may cause suffering. Animal environments in laboratories, zoos and farms need to take this into account as a priority.

In conclusion, the rationale that some forms of life are less valuable than others tends to form a background for much animal research. There have been cases where human participants have been involved in suffering for research (by the Nazis in the Second World War, for instance). There has been debate as to whether the findings of such research can ethically be used. The same surely applies where animal suffering is involved.

Self-Assessment Questions

1. List some of the practical considerations which need to be borne in mind in connection with animal study.
2. What are the important ethical issues which relate to animal study?
3. What answers can be given to those who oppose any use of animals in psychological study?
4. What alternatives exist to the use of animals? Do they seems to you to be viable?

FURTHER READING:

C. J. Lumsden and E. O. Wilson, *Promethean Fire* (Cambridge, Mass. Harvard University Press, 1983).

R. Dawkins, *The Selfish Gene,* 2nd edn (Oxford: Oxford University Press, 1989).

A. Manning and M. Dawkins, *Animal Behaviour,* 4th edn (Cambridge: Cambridge University Press, 1992).

G. Jones, *Social Darwinism and English Thought* (Brighton: Harvester Press, 1980).

Instinct and Learning in the Natural Environment

2

At the end of this chapter you should be able to:

1. Distinguish between phylogeny and ontogeny.
2. Understand and evaluate key terms such as ritualisation, parallel evolution and instinct.
3. Be familiar with the interaction of factors in the decisions made by animals when foraging.
4. Understand and evaluate the importance of early experience in learning situations, such as imprinting, and the interaction of Sign Stimuli with Fixed Action Patterns.
5. Appreciate the role of internal and external factors in the motivation of behaviour.
6. Identify and evaluate factors influencing the motivation of aggression.

SECTION I ADAPTATION TO THE ENVIRONMENT

Introduction

As suggested by Darwin's theory (Chapter 1), adaptation will occur over time, with the result that new species will evolve and existing species will adapt and change, in order to obtain optimum advantage from changing environments; that is to say, to have the greatest chance for genes to survive into succeeding generations. This adaptation of a species over time, by natural selection, is called **phylogenetic adaptation.**

In addition, changes also occur within the lifetime of an individual

31

member of a species. These changes reflect what members of the local population find advantageous and possible. This is known as **ontogenetic adaptation.**

Phylogeny

Evolutionary theory allows for some members of a species not only to evolve into a species distinct from those existing, or those yet to come, but also to continue evolving, as they constantly adapt to the ever-changing pressures of their environment. This differentiation may have benefits, in evolutionary terms, by fitting the new species to a changed environment; for example lower or higher environmental temperatures, the disappearance of a source of food, could mean extinction for that species unless it adapts to these changes. If environmental temperatures decrease, genes which permit tolerance to lower temperatures will survive as opposed to those which do not.

By studying the behaviour patterns of closely related species, it is possible to identify how certain patterns have evolved and where differentiation has occurred. For example, Morris (1959) described evolutionary changes in courtship patterns of tropical grass finches. Male zebra finches, when courting a female, 'bow' forward on their perch and wipe the bill across the perch as though cleaning it. In two related species, the spice finch and the striated finch, the males of both perform the 'bow' and hold the head low over the perch for some seconds, but do not wipe the beak. Morris suggests that the courtship bow of these two species has evolved from an ancestor who did perform beak-wiping during courtship, much as the present-day zebra finch still does. We do not know what change in evolutionary circumstances promoted this differentiation, possibly dietary changes from a sticky to a non-sticky diet, but the innate residual pattern still remained incorporated into the courtship activity.

Ritualisation

An example of evolutionary change was identified by Huxley (1914) and termed **ritualisation**. Ritualisation consists of responses which have no specific function, except to serve as a signal. For instance, Huxley described a component of the courtship display of the great-crested grebe. At one point both partners rise out of the water, presenting nest-building material to each other (see Figure 2.1). While

FIGURE 2.1

The Courtship Display of the Great-Crested Grebe: An Example of Ritualisation

this behaviour derives from elements of the nest-building behaviour of the species, it is not an immediate precursor to nest-building in this context.

Functions of Ritualisation

One of the uses of ritualisation is for members of a species to recognise and respond to signals from other members of the same species;

in this way it can be regarded as a form of communication. (For further discussion of communication, see Chapter 4.) If the initial signal is understood and a 'correct' response is given, the interaction proceeds; if an 'incorrect' response is given, aggression may result (chasing away the intruder, as the individual is now regarded), or even more seriously, in the case of some species of spider, the smaller male spider may be eaten, instead of mated! This illustrates the reason why ritualised responses are timed to a fraction of a second, in order that no mistake is made as to their meaning.

Parallel Evolution

Lorenz (1950) suggested that it would be difficult to identify the origins of many display postures, if these were not identifiable in less ritualised forms in related species. However, we must be careful not to assume that all close similarities in behaviour between species are due to the same causes; they may in fact be due to **parallel evolution**. For example the development of the forelimbs in bats, birds and pterodactyls evolved independently, though each resulted in flight.

Ontogeny

As an animal develops, its behaviour changes. This sub-section examines how this behaviour changes and the extent to which the changes depend on environmental influences. Ontogenic adaptation is closely linked to the causes of these changes. For example, a nestling bird may exhibit behaviours indicative of copulation, which are totally inappropriate for its maturational and motivational state at the time. These behaviours may be regarded in the same light as 'play' behaviours exhibited by mammals: for example, kittens chase and pounce on a toy or small moving object; later in the cat's life those same movements may be used to stalk and capture prey. In the same way, at a later stage in its development, the bird may produce elements of copulatory behaviour, but the full-blown process of copulation requires the coming together of internal and external stimuli.

Internal stimuli for the mating process may include:

- Maturation
- Internal hormonal states

These may need to be prompted by external stimuli such as:

- Extended day-length, as in spring for birds
- Triggers such as warming water, in the case of sticklebacks
- The presence of a sexually available partner.

Successful mating may contribute to the organism's chances of reproduction which, of course, are crucial to the animal's chances of passing on its genes.

Interaction of Genetic and Environmental Factors

The interaction of genetic and enviromental factors can be extremely complex, as shown by Dagan and Volman (1982). A newly-hatched cockroach turns away from a puff of air as accurately as an adult cockroach, in spite of only having four sensory hairs on its cerci instead of 440, as an adult has (a cercus is an antenna-like structure on the cockroach's rear; there are two cerci, one either side: see Figure 2.2). This shows that the fully-fledged response is available from hatching. Yet if an adult loses one of its pair of cerci, its escape behaviour is initially impaired, and it will even turn into the wind instead of away from it. After 30 days, with or without practice, the accurate escape behaviour returns. Somehow its nervous system has altered in order to respond to the remaining intact cercus, demonstrating that adaptation is possible, even after maturation, and even when the fully functional behaviour was available from the time of hatching.

Instinctive behaviour

There was a move in the 1970s to discontinue use of the word **instinct** in comparative psychology, as it had become debased by common usage. Numerous types of behaviour had been loosely or inaccurately described as 'instinctive'. However, tacit agreement seems to have prevailed. The word 'instinctive' is used in its strictly ethological sense as referring to species-specific behaviour which is not controlled by conscious decision-making processes, and has a genetic basis.

An example of species-specific behaviour would be the egg-rolling behaviours of the greylag goose (Lorenz and Tinbergen 1970). If

36

FIGURE 2.2

The Cerci of a Cockroach, used in Detecting Air Movements

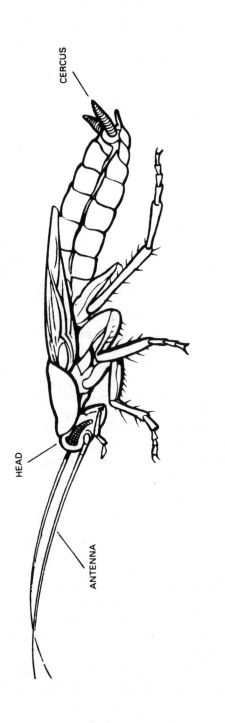

an egg rolls out of the nest of a greylag goose, she stands up and stretches her neck, hooks her beak over it and attempts to roll it back into the nest; even if attempts are unsuccessful she never tries using her feet or wings. Both Lorenz and Tinbergen labelled this behaviour as 'instinctive' but realised that while this was descriptive, it was not sufficiently explanatory. This led to the suggestion that various species evolved **fixed action patterns** (described in Section 2) which are stereotyped behaviour patterns, species-specific and therefore genetically driven.

Cultural Evolution

In most species higher than invertebrates on the **phylogenetic scale** (the scale which suggests how far one species has evolved relative to other species), behaviour is learned from parents, peers or other adults of the same species; not all behaviours are genetically pre-programmed. Many learned behaviours complement instinctive behaviours: for example, in birds the *instinct* to migrate is present, but the young birds learn the *route* to a suitable winter habitat by following the older birds initially. Once learned, this information is then passed on by them to the next generation and the next. Inevitably, minor adaptations to this knowledge have to be made by individuals or generations, as rain forests are cut down or floods wash away deltas. New learning occurs by experience.

This cultural transmission of behaviour occurs among species who have the ability to modify their behaviours. Japanese macaques of Koshuma island were observed picking up sweet potatoes which were caked with earth. One day a female monkey washed her potato in the stream, before eating it. This behaviour was copied by other members of the troop, and the washing of muddy fruit before eating became an established behaviour pattern. This individual monkey had changed the behaviour pattern of her troop; this change may spread to other troops of the same species, or even to related species. In all probability the 'tool-using' behaviour of chimpanzees may have emerged in the same way. Chimps will use a stick to poke into narrow termite holes too small for their hands. When the stick is covered with termites, the chimp will withdraw it from the hole and eat the termites, (McGrew *et al.*, 1979). Chimps of other bands may use grass-stems of leaves instead of twigs. Such behaviour has been observed in a wide range of habitats and the learned behaviour has presumably been available for some time (Schiller, 1957).

The Importance of Parental Care and Lifespan Development

From the above examples it can be seen that species more likely to enlarge their repetoire of behaviours by passing on learned skills are those which

- Form groups
- Have protracted parental care
- Have contact with others of the same species

These learned skills are built on to the genetic components of behaviour. The longer the expected lifespan of an individual, the more they may be expected to learn, and in the higher primates, including humans, learning may appear to overshadow the genetic components of their behaviour. However, there are other constraints. Elephants live longer than chimpanzees, but do not have the same manual dexterity. Their size, strength and bulk also make it less necessary for them to employ stratagems in order to obtain food. Their learning skills, therefore, may only progress as far as is necessary and possible. ('Necessary' begs the question of motivation, which is discussed in Section III.)

The Interplay of Phylogenetic and Ontogenetic Adaptation

As you will have realised by now, there is no fixed and immovable division between behaviour which is genetically driven and that which is learned; what is termed 'instinctive' behaviour is constantly being refined by learning, and much 'learned' behaviour is under-pinned by evolutionary factors. An attempt to divide behaviour between nature and nurture is altogether too simplistic, and not really very useful. What is useful, however, is to have an understanding of the evolutionary basis of behaviour (where it is coming from) and how learning has changed that behaviour, whether through situational constraints or through new opportunities presenting themselves.

Not only vertebrates are capable of learning, of course. The characteristics of learned behaviours in any one species are associated with the needs and instinctive behaviours of that species. The advantage of acquiring a new behaviour through learning is that it assists the individual to survive and/or reproduce successfully, and thereby ensures survival of its genes, or assists the species to move into an ecological niche which is more favourable than the existing one.

Optimal Foraging Theory (OFT)

All animals feed; birds peck, cats pounce and bite, each species feeds in its own specific way. Learned components of behaviour are added to these genetic components. For example, an animal may have to learn *where* is the safest or most fruitful place to feed. These two instances may not be one and the same; where food is most plentiful may not be the safest place. The animal must then make decisions as to what course of action to take in order to maximise what is optimally life-sustaining. It is no use to an individual to go to rich pastures to feed, if the end result is being eaten by a larger predator!

OFT may seem to suggest that a bird foraging in a depleted area may in fact do more for its energy reserves by staying in that area, if the next area for feeding is some distance away. However, before the current patch drops below a viable level (where the energy expended on finding food is not balanced by the poor amount of food found) the bird will make the decision to expend energy and fly to a new site (Krebs and Davies, 1987). It is not known how the animal makes the decision; it is unlikely that it is consciously weighing up the pros and cons, but OFT provides a useful working description of behaviour. Possibly the animal has had previous experience of moving to a new patch if it has failed to find food after a certain length of time, rather than working out travel time and energy losses. (Animals' responses to Schedules of Reinforcement, including time schedules, are outlined in Chapter 3, Section 1.)

In a similar way, humans sometimes behave without conscious thought. For example, if someone throws you a ball, you probably catch it, even if you have no understanding of the laws of physics for flight and aerodynamics. If you stopped to calculate these, you would probably miss the ball!

Various factors influence animals' foraging behaviour, including

- Economic decisions
- Risk-taking
- Food availability.

1. Economic Decisions

Individuals of a species have to make economic decisions when foraging. Bees, for example, have been observed returning to the hive with less than a full load of nectar, even when more was available. Schmid-Hempel *et al.* (1985) found that the further bees had to fly back to the hive, the smaller the load they collected. Full loads were only collected when reasonably close to the hive. In other words, bees were maximising their efficiency by collecting a full load when they could easily manage to transport it to the hive, and a smaller load when they had further to fly, to ensure they had enough strength and stamina for the journey. For starlings, collecting leatherjackets to feed their young, there was a time constraint. Their young needed visiting and feeding frequently. Kacelnik (1984) carried out a series of studies which showed that starlings in fact increased their load size the further they had to fly to their nest. Of course the 'load-weight' which can be carried by bees is a constraining factor, and obviously different from that of a starling's load-to-strength ratio.

2. Risk-Taking Behaviour

Risk-taking behaviour in foraging will increase according to the hunger of the individual. This is why hitherto shy birds are seen on the bird table in winter. Milinski and Heller (1978) found that hungry sticklebacks will accept the danger of lurking predators in order to obtain high intake rates of food. Werner *et al.* (1983) added bass to a pond of bluegill sunfish; the small sunfish were in danger of being eaten by the bass. Subsequent observation showed that the small sunfish only fed in sheltered, low-risk areas, until they grew large enough not to be someone else's dinner. There is clearly a balance to be struck between hunger and the risk of predation.

3. Food Availability

Food availability often shows seasonal variability for many species and behaviour may be adapted accordingly. Territories may be extended in periods of shortage, or even totally changed, as in the case of nomadic habits of herds of antelope or other herbivores. Individuals or groups have to make decisions as to whether it is best to drive away intruders, in order to keep all the available food for themselves, or whether the costs of sharing provide useful benefits, such as providing early warning of, or a distraction to predators. Elgar (1986) studied house sparrows. The first sparrow from a flock to find a food source gives a 'chirrup' call to the remainder of the flock, before flying down to feed. Sparrows in flocks spend less time scanning for predators and consequently more time feeding, therefore the costs of sharing are outweighed by the benefits. But if the food source is indivisible, the individual sparrow does not call the flock, but flies down and feeds alone.

Summary

Phylogeny looks at the changes which take place as species evolve over time, and the emergence of new, related species who may well display common genetic components of behaviour. **Ontogeny** examines the changes which take place within the individuals of a species, during that individual's lifetime. In many species there is interplay between phylogenetic and ontogenetic adaptation, a good example of which is foraging behaviour. The optimal model for foraging behaviour needs to take into account all the **cost** and **benefit** factors such as efficiency, sharing, territoriality, predation risks, food availability and necessary intake levels. Decisions have to be made from second to second. In all cases, there is an element of learning – and frequently, of learning from necessity – imposed upon the instinctual processes whereby animals select prey or feeding sites.

Self-Assessment Questions

1. Identify an example of evolutionary change and describe this in a species.
2. Describe an example of the cultural transmission of behaviour.
3. Discuss how animals make decisions when foraging.

SECTION II   DEVELOPMENT OF BEHAVIOUR WITHIN THE INDIVIDUAL

Early Experience

The importance of early experience in the young organism, including parental care in species where this occurs, makes it essential that the young recognise the parent who will be responsible for them. (We shall be returning to this in Chapter 5.) While there may be genetic elements in this recognition, Lorenz (1952) showed that, in birds and poultry at least, this recognition occurs through an **imprinting** process which takes place early in the new organism's life. Imprinting provides for the

- feeding
- protection
- warmth
- comfort
- early learning

of the young of a species. It ensures a bond between parent and young, usually for a comparatively brief period of time, while parental care is necessary for the above factors.

Imprinting

Lorenz demonstrated in a series of experiments that young birds will follow a stimulus which is presented to them immediately after hatching. This, in the normal run of events, would be the parent bird, but these experiments included a range of unlikely articles such as an orange balloon, as well as Lorenz himself. The essential elements to imprinting on any of these objects were, Lorenz suggested,

1. that they moved (inanimate objects were on a turntable);
2. that they should be presented within 24 hours of hatching; this was called the **critical period:**
3. that imprinting was irreversible once it had taken place.

Lorenz also suggested that imprinting would later influence the choice of sexual partners for mating, but this secondary purpose of imprinting has been called into question by other researchers, for a number of reasons. For example, in a species which exhibits **sexual dimorphism** (where males and females are different in size or colouration), females would expect to mate with other females on maturity, if imprinting had influenced the choice of partners.

Critical/Sensitive Period

Other researchers, such as Guiton (1959), found that this critical period could be extended if the newly hatched birds were kept in the dark until their exposure to the item on which they were to be imprinted. This called into question the concept of a critical period for learning to occur, and the term was modified to **sensitive period**.

This implies that learning will occur more easily at a specific time, but does not rule out the possibility of it ever occurring outside a time as specific as the critical period. The concept of critical period was applied to human bonding, by researchers such as Bowlby (see Chapter 5), but needed to be modified in the light of subsequent research such as Guiton's. In addition, humans have greater powers of rationalisation and cognition than other animals, and are therefore more likely to be able to overcome deficits in early experience. The idea of a critical or sensitive period was thought to have implications for human learning, in that children who were not given the opportunity to learn to speak, or read, or socialise, at times when children normally do these things, would remain disadvantaged. However, care must be exercised in extrapolating into such a complex area as human learning from such basic beginnings. Many studies have shown that skills can be acquired at later periods in life, probably because humans are very adaptable, and also because motivation plays such a large part in human learning.

Components of Imprinting

Hess (1972) carried out a series of experiments, to try to clarify the essential components of imprinting.

1. His first experiment identified that a moving object was necessary (as Lorenz had already suggested); ducklings would follow a model of a female mallard on a turntable when it was set in motion.

2. He found that as well as the visual stimulus of a moving object, there were also auditory components to imprinting; ducklings would follow a quacking model of a male mallard, on a turntable, in preference to a silent model of a female. (Male and female mallards can be differentiated by plumage; the female is cryptic brown, while the male is more colourful, with blue, green and white flashes.)

3. Hess used field studies (1972), as well as laboratory experiments, and found that sound responses in mallards begin *before hatching*, between mother and incubating ducklings. Pre-hatching sounds may facilitate the recognition of maternal calls which are given after hatching. Early imprinting experiments did not include this auditory experience. Imprinting on humans may have occured more easily, as the visual stimulus took on an enhanced importance, in the absence of appropriate auditory stimuli. In addition the only sounds available were human ones. The need to control the variables (hatching birds in incubators, for example, in order to control conditions) may actually have constituted deprivation and thereby confounded the results. In this instance, preliminary field studies could point the way for increased accuracy in laboratory experiments.

4. Hess also found that although imprinting could occur within one hour of hatching, it was at its strongest between 12 and 17 hours after hatching. If no dark-rearing was involved, imprinting was unlikely to occur if no stimulus was presented within 32 hours.

5. The phenomenon of laboratory imprinting was found to be reversible. Ducklings who had imprinted on a human were subsequently allowed to follow a female mallard. After an hour and a half they showed no signs of following a human being again. When the experiment was tried the other way around, there was no transfer; the ducklings did not follow a human, once imprinting had occurred on the female mallard.

Hess therefore proposed that imprinting was most likely to occur when the bird was strong enough to move around and follow the parent, but before the fear of large moving objects developed. Both auditory and visual components are important; auditory stimulation may occur before hatching. Laboratory imprinting may be reversed; imprinting in the natural environment is likely to be irreversible.

Functions of Imprinting

Obvious functions of imprinting are

1. to ensure that the young of a species knows whom to follow for food,
2. where to retreat for warmth or protection.
3. There may be some truth in Lorenz's suggestion that for some species the imprinted model may serve as a model for mating, on achieving maturity.

In addition, imprinting may prepare the young for recognising kin or siblings. These individuals would then not be subject to aggression as might others of the same, or a similar, species. Holmes and Sherman (1982) showed that ground squirrels recognised as 'siblings' those who were reared with them in the nest. This discrimination continued into adulthood. This illustrates the importance of learning in early experience, but imprinting is not the only mechanism in use. There also seems to be some kind of 'phenotype matching' available, as litter mates who were full sisters (same mother, same father) were more co-operative and less aggressive to each other than half-sisters (same mother, but different fathers, due to multiple mating).

These complex recognition patterns indicate it is unlikely that imprinting is the whole story of how one individual recognises another. Imprinting is not a full learning process, but is more accurately viewed as a preparedness for learning. Even then, as Guiton's and others' experiments have shown, it is an **adaptable preparedness**, which enables the individual to adapt to changed environments.

Maturation

Maturation is the biological process through which any organism progresses to become an adult of its species. Biological maturation is an inevitable process, though it is sometimes hindered by insufficient nutrition or forestalled by premature death. The organism does not have to work towards maturity. Maturity is genetically pre-programmed to occur, although individual rates of achieving maturity may vary between individuals of a particular species, owing to intervening variables such as food availability.

As the young of any species matures, behaviours which were present from birth mature into their adult pattern; for example, the type of 'play' aggression directed previously at litter mates becomes the full-blown response, now directed at a potential intruder.

External environmental opportunities may interact with the internal changes brought about by maturation. For example, as the young animal matures, hormonal and other biological changes occur within the body, promoting growth and, later, reproduction. External stimuli such as warmer weather and longer day length may interact with the ability to produce hormones necessary for the reproductive process to take place, but until maturation, day length and warmer weather will not have this effect.

Behaviour Patterns and External Stimuli

Early ethologists such as Tinbergen and Lorenz identified species-specific behaviour patterns in which there were few if any variations between individuals of a species. This lack of variation showed them to be genetically programmed and so they were termed **Fixed Action Patterns (FAPs).**

Lorenz (in Lorenz and Tinbergen, 1970) suggested that FAPs possessed specific characteristics; these were defined by Lea (1984) as follows:

(a) **Universality**
    FAPs occur in all members of a defined group within a species. For example, nesting geese display the egg-rolling behaviour mentioned in Section I, but goslings, ganders and non-nesting geese do not. Egg-rolling is therefore a FAP of nesting geese.

(b) **Stereotyping**
    The behaviour always occurs in the same form, with a small allowance for variation.

(c) **Independent of individual experience**
    If a member of a species is reared in isolation its fixed action patterns will not be significantly different from any other members of the same species.

(d) **Ballisticness**
    Even if circumstances change once the response is initiated, the response itself will not change.

(e) **Single purpose response**
    Each FAP has only one function and is not adapted or used

for any other similar or different purpose. For example the actions involved in egg-rolling are not used by the greylag goose for any other purpose.

(f) **Identifiable trigger stimuli**
There is a specific stimulus or set of stimuli which reliably trigger a specific FAP.

Some FAPs have the rigid quality which Lorenz describes. For example the 'head-throw' of the goldeneye drake, used in courtship rituals, has an average time of 1.29 seconds and variations of only hundreths of a second occur between individuals of the species (Dane *et al.*, 1959). However, while not all behaviour patterns are so rigid in their display and timing, they are still easily recognisable by others of the species. For this reason the more neutral term 'behaviour patterns' is used in descriptions nowadays.

Marler demonstrated by his experiments with white-crowned sparrows that a sub-species might modify or add to a basic FAP. Learned regional variations were added to the basic song pattern (FAPs) of sparrows in various areas along the Pacific coast of the United States.

Sign Stimuli

Many behaviour patterns need a specific external stimulus as a trigger; the 'gape' of a nestling bird is the stimulus for the parent bird to regurgitate or feed the young. Triggers such as this have been termed **Sign Stimuli**. They can be of two kinds:

1. **Excitatory**, promoting behaviour, as in the case of the nestlings, whose gaping beaks prompt the parent to feed them, or
2. **Inhibitory**, as in the case of young turkey chicks,who constantly emit a high-pitched sound which prevents the mother from killing them. This is an aural sign-stimulus. Deaf turkeys may kill their young (Schleidt *et al.*, 1960), because the mother does not hear the appropriate signal (cheeping), and responds with aggression. The excitatory and positive visual stimulus of young turkeys (actually being able to see her young) is ignored in the absence of the inhibitory auditory stimulus, and the young are killed as though they do not belong to her.

Attributes of Sign Stimuli

Tinbergen (1950) studied sticklebacks to find out what stimuli encouraged the male to mate with a female, and to drive other males away from his territory. Using a series of experimental stimuli he showed that the red underbelly of the male was the stimulus to attack, whilst the swollen (grey-brown) underbelly of a female was the stimulus for mating. Even when they were **supernormal stimuli** (that is to say, exaggerated stimuli which are more effective than normal stimuli in eliciting a response), the specific behaviours were still elicited. A red underbelly (however large) still provoked attack, while an abnormally large 'female' underbelly promoted repeated enthusiastic attempts at mating. Rowland (1989) demonstrated that a male stickleback directed courtship to a 'dummy' female with an abnormally large abdomen in preference to a 'dummy' female of normal proportions. In the real-life situation, courting the fattest female would result in more eggs laid in the male's nest, thereby optimising his chances of passing on his genes. In the same way, if a greylag goose is presented with a much larger (but correctly coloured) egg outside her nest, the goose will attempt to retrieve it by egg-rolling.

This may cast some light on the question of why host birds will accept cuckoo eggs, which are often larger than their own, and the cuckoo nestling, which is often larger than the 'adoptive parents' themselves.

Displacement activities

As Tinbergen (1951) has described, recognisable behaviour was sometimes seen to occur in totally irrelevant contexts or situations. For example, an animal might break off from a threat display and begin to preen, or a male stickleback who has been attempting unsuccessfully to court a female, might break off his activities and swim to his nest-site, performing the 'fanning' movements with which he would ventilate eggs in the nest – except that the eggs have not been laid! This type of 'irrelevant' behaviour Tinbergen called a **displacement activity.**

It has been suggested that stress or conflict causes displacement activities. Rowell (1961) suggested they occur when the animal is in a protracted conflict situation and inappropriate responses may be made. It has also been suggested that extremes of displacement activities can be produced in animals suffering severe stress or conflict, such as the bar-biting exhibited by sows in farrowing crates and the head-swinging movements of polar bears and elephants in captivity. In the natural situation there is usually an escape route from severe conflict; appeasement gestures can be offered, or flight, to terminate fights, or a new mate can be found if courtship does not proceed. Displacement activities may simply fulfil the function of breaking off an unsuccessful pattern of behaviour and giving the animal time and space to find an appropriate response.

Approach/Avoidance Conflict

When a conflict of motives occurs, between, say, the need to gain access to food or water and something which gets in the way of satisfying that need (another animal, perhaps), then an animal will be in a state of stress. Time is needed for the animal to gather information so as to come to a decision. When there is an encounter between one animal and another internal conflict may arise as to whether flight or attack is the best course. There may not be sufficient information immediately available about the other animal's fighting capacity or willingness to fight. In these circumstances displacement activity may occur. Masserman (1950) attempted to produce stress experimentally. Cats, trained to open a box for food, sometimes received a strong blast of air. Their behaviour became quite disturbed. Some became hysterical, others became depressed. Physiologically they showed all the signs of acute stress, raised blood pressure, gastric problems and hair erection.

Vacuum Activities

When the normal activities towards which animals are motivated are frustrated by the absence of suitable stimuli animals may engage in **vacuum activity**. That is to say, they may still engage in what amounts to FAPs, even though the appropriate trigger for these patterns is missing. A hen would normally engage in dustbathing (scratching out and then wallowing in a patch of bare earth or dust). Even when confined to a cage with a wire floor the hen may go through the motions of scratching and wallowing. Vestergaard (1980) called this vaccuum dustbathing. This animal is displaying very high motivation to perform a frustrated activity.

Displacement Activities Among Human Beings

Morris (1977) in his book *Manwatching: A Field Guide to Human Behaviour* describes how humans engage in displacement activities under stress:

> Social occasions are, not surprisingly, riddled with displacement interjections. The host as he crosses the room, is rubbing his hands together (displacement handwashing); one of his guests is carefully smoothing her dress (displacement grooming); the hostess is shifting some magazines (displacement tidying); another guest is stroking his beard (displacement grooming again); the host is preparing drinks and the guests are sipping them (displacement drinking); the hostess is offering round small tidbits and the guests are nibbling them (displacement eating). (Morris, 1977, p. 180).

Have you ever combed your hair, tied a shoelace, lit a cigarette, not because you needed to do these things but simply because you felt embarrassed or did not know how to respond to someone, and needed time to gather your thoughts?

Physiological Concomitants of Stress and Frustration

Stress may result from a variety of causes including frustration, overcrowding, extremes of temperature or the inability to escape from a position of apparent danger. Fraser and Broom (1990), in describing the physiological changes which accompany stress, point out that most are attempts to restore the delicate balance of the animal's metabolism.

Moderate Stress

In cases of moderate stress the activity of the autonomic nervous system is heightened. Adrenalin is released and other physiological changes take place:

- Sweat glands of the skin begin to secrete.
- Hair becomes erected.
- There is an increase in heart rate.
- Breathing becomes more rapid.
- Blood is redistributed towards the muscles.

These physiological changes apply not just to conflict situations but also where there is strong arousal, attack, escape, sex.

More Severe or Persistent Stress

Where the stressful situation persists, adrenocorticotrophic hormone (ACTH) is released by the pituitary gland, which prompts the adrenal cortex to release steroids. Under chronic stress animals may suffer from gastric ulcers, loss of hair or tumours of the pituitary gland; they may become ill eough to die.

In the natural environment there is nearly always the option of escape from a conflict situation as a last resort. The physiological results of prolonged stress do not seem to be adaptive and no mechanism exists to deal with chronic conflict. Animals in captivity or human beings, however, may find themselves the victims of chronic stress or conflict.

Conflict and Display

In some cases the conflicts which occur are connected to display. Red deer may remain in a state of conflict, for example, while an assessment is made of an opponent's ability to fight. Roaring and walking up and down are part of the assessment process for stags. When a stag hears his opponent producing a high number of roars per minute he will assume his adversary is fit and strong and may retreat. The conflict situation will not persist.

Threat and Appeasement

Darwin (1872) described what he called the **principle of antithesis.** A species may exhibit two completely opposed postures to members of the same species. The first is the **threat posture** and the second the **appeasement posture.** Tinbergen (1959) has illustrated these postures in relation to the lesser black-backed gull. In the threat posture the bird moves towards its rival with its neck stretched upwards and forwards, its bill and head pointing down and its wings lifted clear of the body; its plumage is slightly raised. The appeasement posture is almost the complete antithesis.The head is held low and the bill points upwards. The wings are pressed close to the body. There is no way in which the bird is going to engage in attacking its opponent, which would involve beating with its wings and attempting to peck down on him.

Evolutionary Stable Strategies (ESS)

Maynard-Smith (1982) developed a 'game theory' approach to these problems. This implies that an animal will develop strategies which have the best chance of enhancing life expectancy and reproductive capacity. Once an aggressor has received an appeasement signal from his opponent his best strategy is to call off the fight. After all, if the fight continues there is the risk (albeit a small one) that he will lose, or else the greater risk that he may receive injury such as to impair his life expectancy or reproductive chances.

Furthermore, while he is engaged in the fight, time and energy are being lost which could more profitably be spent gathering food or protecting mates. Appeasement in the face of a stronger rival or the acceptance of appeasement from a weaker one is likely to confer an advantage in terms of passing on one's genes to the next generation. The genes which determine this behaviour rather than fighting on in the face of damage and injury are more likely to be successful. Only if aggression can be carried through without serious risk would it be to the advantage of the individual not to accept appeasement if offered, or not to offer it in the face of greater strength. Evolutionary stability is unlikely to result either from consistently aggressive or from consistently subservient behaviour.

Complex Situations

Sign stimuli and resultant behaviour patterns may be adequate in simple situations, but where decisions have to be made the direct responses may have to be adapted or modified. For example, Seeley (1985) describes the complex assessments of honey-bee scouts looking for new quarters. Premises are only considered suitable if they conform to a number of prerequisites. For instance, the volume of the cavity has to be between 15 and 80 litres, it has to have a south-facing entrance, smaller than 75 square centimetres, the nest site needs to be several metres above groundand between 100 and 400 metres from the parent nest. Seeley showed that the scout walked round and round the interior to assess its cavity. All other factors must also be weighed up and co-ordinated.

Davies and Brooke (1989) found that species which are currently host to cuckoo eggs (reed warblers, meadow pipits and pied wagtails) showed some degree of discrimination between their own eggs and model eggs. If the model eggs were similar to their own they would be accepted. Consequently different cuckoos specialised in different hosts and laid eggs similar to their chosen hosts (see Figure 2.3). Some species, such as flycatchers and reed buntings, would also make suitable hosts, as they have similar diets and nesting sites, but are not parasitised by cuckoos. These species, when tested, rejected all model eggs. Davies and Brooke suggest that they were once parasitised by cuckoos but their egg-discrimination skills became so good, they were no longer used as hosts. On the other hand, species which are no use to cuckoos, by virtue of unsuitable diet or location, appear not to have sophisticated egg-discrimination skills.

It would seem that while the basic genetic sign-stimuli prompts remain fairly consistent, when circumstances demand there can be many kinds of modification. Learning plays a part not just in the individual's behaviour, but in that of the entire species.

Self-Assessment Questions

1. What are the processes and functions of imprinting? Support your answer with appropriate evidence from studies.
2. Define and give examples of (a) Sign Stimuli, (b) Fixed Action Patterns, (c) Displacement Activities.
3. Describe an example of a genetically-programmed component of behaviour which has been modified to accommodate a complex situation.
4. What are meant by evolutionary stable strategies? Describe an example of ESS.

SECTION III MOTIVATION

Motivation is an issue central to psychology. It examines why people and animals do the things they do, why they perform one specific activity rather than another, and what makes them change from one activity to another. Neural, hormonal and environmental factors are involved.

54

FIGURE 2.3

Examples of Birds' Eggs Mimicked by Cuckoos

REED WARBLER · MEADOW PIPIT · PIED WAGTAIL · DUNNOCK · WREN

Top row: Cuckoo eggs from a reed warbler nest, meadow pipit nest and pied wagtail nest.
Bottom row: Eggs from species often parasitised by cuckoos. From left to right: reed warbler pipit, pied wagtail, sedge warbler, robin. (Note size difference, showing lack of discrimination in host birds).

There are several theoretical positions associated with motivation. One dichotomy is whether behaviour is **homeostatically or non-homeostatically motivated.**

Homeostatic Motivation

The word 'homeostasis' was used by Cannon, in the 1920s, to describe the body's striving to maintain its physiological balance, in spite of internal and external changes. An example of a homeostatic motivation is hunger. The recognition by the body that food has to be taken in, in order to maintain its body weight, prompts the behaviour of eating. Of course, other factors may play a role in this recognition and subsequently produce aberrant behaviours such as overeating or under-eating (leading to anorexia in humans).

Non-Homeostatic Motivation

Other motivated behaviours, such as play and curiosity, are exhibited by a number of species as well as humans. These cannot be regarded as directly life-preserving, and therefore not homeostatic. They must have explanations other than physiological necessity.

In addition to the two dimensions of homeostatic or non-homeostatic motivation, there are also the roles played by **internal** and **external stimuli.**

Externally Stimulated Motivation

Changes in day length and temperature in the springtime may encourage mating behaviours to commence in birds; this is where the external environment is influencing instinctive behaviour. Alternatively, the establishment of an animal's own territory may promote aggression towards another of the same species. On neutral territory this would not be exhibited – in fact avoidance might be the order of the day.

Internally Stimulated Motivation

The internal environment of animals is largely influenced by their hormonal systems. While some hormonal changes are prompted by external changes or **triggers** (such as the production of springtime mating behaviour, mentioned above) others are cyclical. Hunger and thirst, for instance, are regular occurrences prompted by bodily changes, which are recognised by internal mechanisms. These drives aim to maintain the organism's body in a steady state, and serve to preserve the organism itself. Sexual behaviour cannot be seen as homeostatic in the same way, but is seen as instrumental in passing on the individual's genes.

Interaction of Internal and External Stimuli

There is a necessity for external and internal stimuli to be available together, in order that behaviour will occur appropriately. However hungry, the animal cannot feed if the external stimulus of food is unavailable. Other forms of behaviour require the coming-together of internal states and external motivators.

Theories of Motivation

1. Homeostatic Theories

(a) Drive Theories

Goal-oriented behaviour was studied by the early ethologists, such as Lorenz and Tinbergen. They tried to interpret and simplify the relationship between internal and external environmental motivations by use of a concept which they called 'drives'. A hunger drive, or mating drive, or aggressive drive was seen to build up through lack of the appropriate activity. When sufficient build-up had accumulated the drive would be released and the behaviour would be exhibited; hunger drive by eating, aggressive drive by fighting, and so on. However, this does not explain why a cat who is not hungry will stalk mice; you have probably noticed that your domestic cat will kill them and bring them home – for you?

Lorenz's Psychohydraulic Model

Lorenz (1950) proposed the **psychohydraulic model** (see Figure 2.4). He drew an analogy between water filling a tank, reaching a high level (representing what he called **action-specific energy**) and the resultant pressure making the water flow out, representing the

FIGURE 2.4

Diagram of the Psychohydraulic Model of Motivation Proposed by Lorenz (1950)

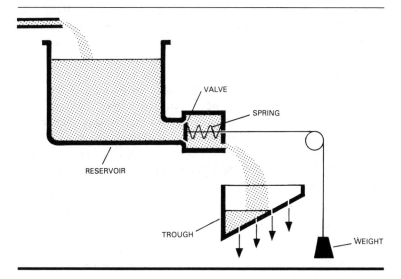

subsequent **behaviour**. For example, hunger can be viewed as a need-induced drive; action-specific energy is the motivation to produce a specific behaviour which would alleviate that hunger. Depending on the need, there may be a choice of behaviours or FAPs which would be appropriate. According to the theory, a behaviour would not occur again until the action-specific energy had built up again. Lorenz also used this model to explain displacement activities; the pressure to display a certain behaviour was strong, but the behaviour was unacceptable or frustrated at that time. The pressure therefore forced a substitute behaviour to be exhibited.

However, in a number of instances, it was pointed out that observed behaviour does not always tie in with the theory. To take a specific example, if we consider hunger as a need promoting an action-specific energy, it is alleviated by feeding. However, Janowitz and Grossman (1949) showed that if food is placed directly into the stomach of a hungry dog, the behaviour of feeding stops; there is no necessity for the animal to continue its behaviour. Lorenz's model does not allow for feedback from the environment.

Hull's General Drive Theory

Hull's General Drive Theory (1943) incorporated the concept of **need** (see Figure 2.5). A need promoted a drive, which in turn led to the appropriate behaviour. On receiving feedback from this activity, the need ceases and with it the drive and the behaviour. Yet even this is not a full explanation; an animal will cease feeding before it receives physiological signals that its stomach is full.

However, neither Hull's nor Lorenz's models can explain motivations such as curiosity, play, or risk-taking behaviours, which are often highly arousing. If you have never climbed Everest, according to these early theories you should be suffering an uncontrollable desire to get up there at once! Other Drive theories, such as that of Mowrer, 1950, or Deutsch (1960), proposed amendments which still failed to explain motivated behaviour which was not simple cause-and-effect.

Other Homeostatic Models

Homeostatic models such as McFarland's (1971) and Toates (1986) bear some similarities to drive theory, in that they see the hungry or thirsty animal as motivated to eat or drink in order to maintain its body; piloerection (hair standing on end, or 'goosepimples' in humans) maintains the body-temperature even when the environmental temperature falls. Negative feedback provides the motivation to switch off the behaviour when there is no longer any need.

Feedforward

The Homeostatic Model also fails to explain the phenomenon of **feedforward**, observed by McFarland (1971). An animal will drink extra in anticipation of a thirst, or eat more than whatever is just life-sustaining in anticipation of a 'hungry' period. Simple cause-and-effect mechanisms are inadequate explanations for such motivated behaviour.

Evaluation of Homeostatic Theories

The body's homeostatic responses are brought about automatically, often through the animal's autonomic nervous system. You yourself

FIGURE 2.5
Diagramatic Representation of Hull's General Drive Theory

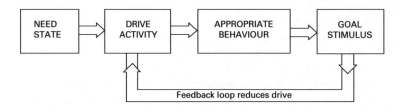

do not have to think 'I am cold, I will produce goosepimples.' However, many of the behavioural *responses* are voluntary (for example, eating). Homeostasis is more than a simple cause-and effect mechanism. A thirsty animal is thirsty because its extracellular fluids are diminished and its body cells are dehydrated. But while there is a considerable time-lag between a drink being taken and actually reaching the animal's body cells, it does not continue drinking during that time lag. Miller *et al.* (1957) showed that the mouth and oesophagus of rats contain water detectors which may serve to measure water intake and cut off drinking behaviour. The ultimate 'effect' is estimated before cells are rehydrated. Similar activity happens with food and eating.

In addition, according to the Homeostatic Model, once animals have eaten enough, they should not eat again until digested food has passed through the system and hunger has built up once more. In fact, Wirtschafter and Davis (1977) found that rats who were offered a wider variety of food than normal, would eat excessively and possibly become obese. Obviously external stimuli (the sight and smell of novel foods) made the rats exceed their normal intake which would have been prompted by their internal messages. This may highlight one of the many possible reasons for human obesity, the availability of attractive foods in large quantities. In addition, both animals and humans possess the ability to assess when food is likely to be in short supply in the future, and to eat extra in anticipation. This cannot be viewed as a homeostatic response mechanism, therefore other mechanisms must be involved.

2. Non-Homeostatic Theories

If homeostatic motivation is basic to life-sustaining behaviour for the individual, what explanations are there for non-homeostatic behaviour, such as sexual behaviour, play or curiosity? Neural factors, hormonal levels and other physiological mechanisms which feature largely in homeostatic motivation, may also contribute to other forms of motivation. When rats are placed in a strange maze they will spend some time exploring their new environment, without any reward being offered them. It has been suggested this could be potentially life-saving, in that, should a threat appear, they would know where to escape. If no escape is available, they would know it would be best to use the freezing response, to avoid detection, whereas naive rats would run to look for escape and probably be caught (Blanchard *et al.* 1976). Harlow (1950) observed that monkeys would solve puzzles and carry out tasks solely for the reward of being allowed to watch other monkeys through a window. As far as one can tell, there was no intrinsic benefit to the watchers; they did not learn potentially life-saving behaviour by watching the others, and watching served no homeostatic function.

Arousal Theory

Some forms of animal behaviour, such as play and curiosity, may possibly be explained by the Arousal Theory of motivation. Arousal has been defined as a mental state of readiness for activity. Low arousal may indicate a bored or drowsy state, while very high arousal may convey panic or hysteria. Arousal theory suggests that animals, including humans, are constantly seeking an optimum level of arousal. An animal which is constantly involved in food-seeking behaviour is unlikely to exhibit curiosity, because its arousal level is already maintained and fulfilled. Given that there is no homeostatic value in curiosity, is it simply a behaviour which occurs in a vacuum, to fill time? Certainly it seems to occur mainly when homeostatic balance has been achieved, but not all animals exhibit curiosity, or sensation-seeking, when homeostatic functions are satisfied. Other factors not yet identified must be involved.

Self-Stimulation of the Brain

Olds and Milner (1954) found that there were instances where animals became so motivated to carry out a behaviour that homeostatic motivations were ignored. Researchers implanted an electrode in what became known as the Pleasure Centre of the rat's brain. The rat was able to stimulate that part electrically, by pressing a bar. Some rats continued to press the bars until they were exhausted, ignoring food, drink and sexually receptive females. The researchers assumed that the rats were performing the activity for pleasure, which is why that area of the brain was dubbed the pleasure centre.

Other Theories of Motivation

Perhaps we should be discussing motivation as a hierachy, rather than as a unitary concept. Maslow (1970) proposed a hierachy of needs, in his theory of motivation (see Figure 2.6). Basic needs to be satisfied first are physiological: food, drink, shelter, safety. Progression through the hierachy is achieved until the pinnacle of self-actualisation, which sounds appropriate for humans, but difficult to envisage in animal terms. Neither are Psychoanalytic, Cognitive or other Humanistic theories of motivation applicable within the context of this book. These are discussed in 'Perspectives in Psychology' by Malim, Birch and Wadeley (1992). However self-stimulation of the brain does not fit any of the models or theories so far discussed.

The Motivation of Sexual Behaviour

Sexual behaviour in itself is not regarded as a homeostatic mechanism, as it does nothing to maintain the individual, though it does contribute to passing on the individual's genes. It does not therefore fit the homeostatic model, although it may fit the concept of drive. As mentioned at the start of this section, internal and external factors often need to come together to promote sexual behaviour in many species. Such factors include the external advent of spring and a sexually available partner, plus internal physiological readiness, such as changed hormonal states and neural factors (see Box 2.1

FIGURE 2.6
Maslow's (1970) Hierarchy of Needs Model of Motivation

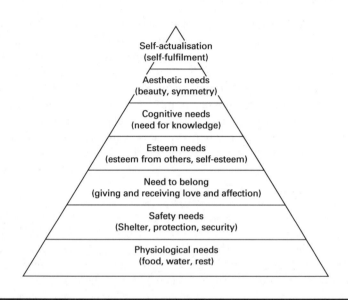

at the end of this chapter). Specific areas of the brain are thought to contribute to sexual behaviours in many species; these are sometimes different areas for male and female of the same species. In humans and some animals the picture is even more complex, with the cognitive elements of 'liking' or the intangible elements of 'loving' superimposed; there may be similar elements in the pair-bonding of some animal species, such as swans who mate for life.

Motivation for Maternal/Paternal Behaviours

Parenting cannot be viewed as a homeostatic mechanism, in that it does not serve to maintain the individual offering the behaviour (quite the reverse, some parents would say!) But, like sexual behaviour, it does serve to pass on the individual's genes.

Paternal behaviour does not appear in all species; in higher primates and many birds, parenting is the responsibility of both male and female, either equally or unequally. In some species of fish, for example sticklebacks, the male builds the nest, incites the female to deposit her eggs, then fertilises them and defends them until hatching. Unfortunately the neural mechanisms of such parental behaviour have not been well-researched as yet. Predominance has been given to research on maternal behaviour, especially rodents (see Box 2.1) as they are easier to investigate in laboratories.

Nest-building behaviour in rats or mice has been found to be prompted by changes in hormonal levels. The initiation of maternal behaviour in rats is prompted by olfaction (the smell of the pups); of secondary importance is the sight and the sounds they make.

Motivation for Aggression

One of the areas of motivation much studied by ethologists is that of the motivation for aggression; obviously there are implications for the better understanding of human aggression the more understanding we have of other species.

In animals other than humans, some main functions of aggression have been identified. These include

- defence of territory
- competition for mates
- defence of own offspring
- status in the social order of the species.

Whilst these may well be applicable to humans, human motivational processes are more complex and difficult to analyse.

Aggressive behaviour can take different forms, for different reasons, but can roughly be divided into three main areas: offensive, defensive and predatory. These are controlled by different brain mechanisms, which would seem to confirm them as separate mechanisms which are related behaviourally although they do not follow identical patterns (see Box 2.1, pp. 73–5).

Environmental Influences on Aggression

Environmental influences shown to increase aggression include

- overcrowding
- isolation
- territorial changes.

Overcrowding: In both laboratory and field studies, overcrowding has been shown to be linked with aggression. Calhoun (1962) found that laboratory rats who were living in overcrowded conditions were more aggressive than rats of the same strain who had ample space. Pulliam (1976) and Caraco *et al.* (1980) observed that as the size of flocks of yellow-eyed junco increased, so did the proportion of time spent in aggression.

Isolation: Where animals have been kept in total isolation they have been found to be very aggressive. Kruijt (1964) found this to be the case with jungle fowl, where after months of isolation birds would even resort to long battles with their tails.

Territory: A frequent cause of aggression between animals is the defence of territory. This is often carried out as a precursor to mating behaviour; in the case of the stickleback as a place for the courted female to lay her eggs. Hawks and many other birds defend their territories in order to safeguard their supply of food. Other species defend their territories for food, courtship areas or places to rear their young. Baboons are nomadic, but defend their temporary territories against intruders until food stocks are depleted, before moving on to a new area.

While one's own territory will always be defended, from time to time an animal needs to expand its territory; for instance, in winter food may not be so readily available, so the animal needs to range wider, causing conflicts with neighbours, who may also be seeking to expand their territories.

Definitions of aggression in human terms tend to look only at offensive aggression, as though defensive and predatory behaviours do not exist. Yet current thinking on the increasing problem of aggression among car-drivers suggests that it is a defensive reaction, defending one's personal (road) space. In speaking of wars, defence of territory is viewed as permissible, even laudable, but not road space. By looking at examples of animal aggression we can remove the moral and cultural complications, which render some of the definitions of aggression inadequate when applied to humans.

Physiological Factors

Whether an animal wins or loses an altercation, the body's responses are the same. In aggression the same mechanisms are involved as during stress (described in the previous section); when aggression or stress subsides the body's responses return to baseline again (homeostasis). Balance is restored in the Autonomic Nervous System and the hormonal system.

High adrenalin levels and high testosterone levels are hormones implicated in aggressiveness. Many studies have shown that a high level of testosterone, the male hormone, is implicated in aggression. Albert *et al.* (1989) demonstrated that castrated male rats treated with testosterone fought and dominated other male castrates who were untreated.

It has been suggested that specific brain areas are involved in aggressive behaviour, as with other forms of motivation. Again, these may not only be different from one species to the next, but between male and female of the same species.

Is Aggression Innate?

Lorenz, in his book *On Aggression* (1966), defined aggression as 'the fighting instinct in beast and man which is directed against members of the same species'. It is useful for our purposes that we confine aggression to attacks on members of the *same* species. The problem many ethologists and others have with Lorenz's definition is that the word 'instinct' implies it is innate and genetically pre-programmed into us – man and beast. While many people will accept it is in the 'beast', they prefer to think of 'man' as having free will.

Lorenz suggested that an individual of a species avoids a fight to the death with another of the same species, through the recognition of **appeasement gestures** which inhibit the final death blow, as the death of an individual would be detrimental to the species by diminishing the gene pool. For example, dogs will roll on to their backs, exposing their soft underbelly and the vulnerable part of the throat; this action says 'I give in.' In humans, cringing, pleading, smiling or crying act as appeasement gestures. Although humans do not have large canine teeth or other equipment for killing others of the same size of the same species, their cognitive abilities are advanced enough to devise weapons for that purpose. Lorenz's claim that an animal's aggression stops short of killing it's own species has been undermined by numerous studies. Lea (1984) points out that infanticide is one of the more common forms of aggression among animals; instances among lions are well documented. Goodall (1968) reported warfare among two bands of chimpanzees which resulted in the death of all adult males from one band. It would appear therefore that irrespective of appeasement gestures, provision or lack of physical weapons to kill, the killing of animals of the same species does occur. Whether this is innately pre-programmed, or culturally devised and learned, has not been clearly demonstrated.

Post-Aggression Recess?

Lorenz's psychohydraulic model of motivation would suggest that after a fight or aggressive behaviour, there would be less motivation on the part of the animal to exhibit aggressive behaviour again for some time. Conversely, in the absence of opportunities for aggressive behaviour, aggression would build up within the individual, to be released at the first opportunity. In fact the reverse of both these extremes has been found by a number of researchers. Heilingberg and Kramer (1972) tested an aggressive species of cichlid fish (called Pelmatochromis). Males were kept on their own with no opportunity to meet other males, and components of aggressive behaviour diminished over a number of days, rather than building up.

Wilz (1970) found that male sticklebacks would deliver more 'bites' (the measure of aggression used) towards a test-tube containing another male at the end of a ten-minute period than at the beginning. Even when the test-tubed intruder was removed from the territory, the stickleback still showed aggressive behaviour. It even attacked a female (which would not be expected), and seemed unable to respond sexually for some time. However, one could possibly argue that the level of aggression was falsely maintained as the consummatory behaviour of fighting was never achieved, although the intruder was removed eventually, or 'driven away'. The cause of aggression could have shifted from 'territory defence' to 'frustration'.

Irritable Aggression

Irritable aggression caused by pain, anxiety, negative stimuli and frustration, whilst potentially equally as damaging as any other form of aggression, does not serve a function, such as the defence of territory, nor a proximal cause, such as the presence of an intruder.

Frustration is often considered to be a cause of aggression in humans as well as other species, and this may be due to any number of causes. In species which have hierachical social organisations (see Chapter 5), aggression may be due to attempts to rise in the dominance order of the social hierachy. Patterns of aggression shown to potential predators or intruders of other species may contain similar elements to aggressive behaviours within a species, but are not always identical.

Learning and Aggression

A number of studies have shown that early learning affects the level of aggression shown by an individual. Male and female rats reared in isolation are more aggressive than rats of the same strain which have been gently handled by humans when young. Namikas and Wehmer (1978) found that male mice reared in litters with male siblings were less aggressive to other males in adulthood than males who had been reared solely with female siblings.

While it would be most unwise to generalise these findings to humans, there may be implications worthy of attention. The human species has much greater potential for learning than rats – or indeed than any other animal. It also lives longer than most. If there is such a thing as a basic instinct for aggression, perhaps it might be controlled or enhanced by learning. If high levels of testosterone are implicated in human aggression, these are at their highest during adolescence. It could be argued that humans are, by then, socialised enough (through learning) to be able to control or redirect their aggression to some extent. Perhaps those who do not have missed out on a degree of socialisation? Or perhaps their learning suggested to them that aggression was permissible, even laudable (Bandura, 1971)?

Individual Influences in Aggression

Specific factors have been shown to influence the level of aggressive behaviour demonstrated by an individual in a species. These include

- the size of the individual relative to others,
- the size of the animal's natural 'weapons',
- past experiences,
- 'badges' of seniority,
- displays of dominance.

Individual Size   The size of an animal relative to others of its species will often determine whether an animal will initiate an attack. Smaller animals are more likely to offer appeasement gestures or run away.

Natural Weapons   Likewise the size of an animal's natural 'weapons' (horns, antlers, canine teeth) also have bearing on aggressive behaviours.

Past experiences   Past experiences, especially if one individual has previously lost an encounter with the one now offering aggression, is going to affect decisions whether to fight or run away.

Badges of Seniority   'Badges' of seniority are recognised by individuals who live in social groups. However Rohwer (1978) showed that it takes more than just the badge to determine dominance. Dominant birds in flocks of Harris sparrows have dark head and breast feathers. When subordinate birds were painted with black paint, they did not rise in status, because their behaviour did not match their plumage. However when they were also injected with testosterone a change in behaviour was observed along with a rise in status.

Dominance displays   Displays of dominance discourage aggression from others, for example the roar of a stag, or the chest-beating of a male gorilla, actively discourage aggression from others of the species, thereby avoiding the necessity for actual fighting. This is as well, since the assertion that death will be avoided in intraspecies encounters does not always hold true. Wilkinson and Shank (1977) suggested that 5 to 10 per cent of adult musk ox bulls may die each year in fights over females. Stags fight for females during the rutting season; their antlers may inflict wounds which could be fatal. Clutton-Brock *et al.* (1982) observed that two animals of equal size will tend to prolong their fight, neither being willing to give in or offer the appeasement gesture of leaving the arena.

Natural populations of some species differ in their levels of aggression. Maynard-Smith and Riechart (1984) demonstrated that the desert spider (aegelopsis) is very aggressive. They fight over access to web sites. Fear and aggression alternate during encounters between two spiders. Factors involved include ownership of the disputed site, relative bodyweight of the two contestants, quality of the territory involved and genetic factors. Some populations of spiders are more aggressive than others. Even where the external situation is the same, some will withdraw more readily than others.

Evolution of Fighting

The reason that individuals in a species do not fight to the death was suggested by Lorenz to be a mechanism designed to avoid the reduction of the gene pool available to the species. If this were so, one might argue, where was the usefulness in evolving fighting behaviour at all, if it promoted the inevitable risk that some individuals might accidentally be killed, as in the case of the musk ox bulls. The **costs and benefits model** developed by Maynard-Smith (1976) suggest that aggression may be used by an individual if the resultant benefits appear to outweigh the costs. Evolutionary stable strategies (ESS), discussed in the previous section, emerge from the interaction of genetically programmed behaviour plus the animal's experiences in previous similar situations, possibly with the same adversary. The decision to attack or retreat is made. Ecological circumstances such as the availability of food, mates, status or territory and the number of competitors, will determine the pay-offs.

Is Aggression a Male Prerogative?

Research would seem to suggest that the answer to this is yes – or is it that there has been little research into female aggression? Certainly higher levels of androgens (male hormones) seem related to aggres-sive behaviours; these hormones are present in smaller, but varying amounts in females. Vom Saal and Bronson (1980) found that fe-male rats who had been situated between two male siblings in the uterus, had significantly higher levels of testosterone than other females who were next to only one male or all female siblings. When tested as adults, these females showed higher levels of inter-female ag-gression than other rats, although there was no difference in their fertility or maternal behaviour.

Female hamsters are always more aggressive than males. Their aggressiveness does not seem to be hormone-dependent, but is inhibited during oestrus, when both progesterone and estradiol are present. Injections of either hormone alone does not inhibit aggression.

Some primates, such as rhesus monkeys and baboons, become more aggressive around the time of ovulation (Saayman, 1971). In humans, researchers have found that aggressive behaviour decreases around the time of ovulation, but increases prior to menstruation; increased irritability has been noted as a symptom of pre-menstrual tension, which in less-controlled individuals could spill over into acts of aggression. This may be related to hormonal changes prior to menstruation or retention of fluid which causes pressure within the brain.

It is usually the males of the species which have evolved the 'weaponry'. The antlers of the stags, or the large claw of the fiddler crabs, for instance, have evolved by a process of natural selection; the victor of a battle for a female will have passed on his genes, which included those for the growth of large antlers or claws. Fe-males, as the 'resource' in this scenario, had no necessity to evolve these – although they could be useful in defending young. Many cows, female wildebeest and goats have horns, and will use them for this purpose. On the other hand, females of many species co-operate with other females, especially in areas such as rearing young; probably antlers or horns would inhibit this co-operation.

In most species, females with young are aggressive if threatened. Maternal aggressiveness in mice may become apparent during preg-nancy, where it appears to relate to a rise in progesterone levels (Mann *et al.*, 1984). However, these levels drop at parturition. The stimuli for maternal aggression after birth seems to be the sight and the smell of the pups (Svare and Gandelman, 1976). Calhoun

(1962), in his study of overcrowding in rats, identified instances of infanticide by females. Other females known to kill their young include sows, and sometimes cats and dogs. Infanticide is more likely to be carried out by males, as a precursor to impregnating the mother, in order to propagate their own genes. Two reasons have been suggested for female infanticide: to decrease crowding and to attain an optimal litter size.

Female spiders will kill a male who makes a mistake in the courtship pattern, or sometimes after mating, simply as a source of food. However, the female spider of many species is often larger than the male. The female praying mantis does not wait for the male to finish the act of copulation, but bites off his head before the act is finished; reflexes ensure that fertilisation ensues.

In humans, the Amazons, a mythical tribe of women, were reputed to be fierce and warlike (Herodotus, circa 500 BC); as there were no men, women took on the role of warriors, and cut off their right breast, in order to draw a bow. Whether there was any historical evidence for a tribe of aggressive women, or whether it was mere fantasy, we shall probably never know, but the legend serves to suggest that the concept of 'aggressive women' was not viewed as implausible, 2,000 years ago.

Current female aggression is complex and probably culturally and socially influenced; for example female circumcision is carried out by other females, although probably originally instigated by males. Whether female circumcision is an act of aggression can be debated. Certainly there is no hygienic reason, as there is with male circumcision; reasons given seem wholly punitive rather than practical.

We have instanced some examples of female aggression; undoubtedly there are others, although it is the more flamboyant displays of male aggression which are researched more often.

Measuring Motivation

There is no way as yet of measuring motivation, and we can only measure the resultant behaviour; for example we can count the rate of bar-pressing or key-pecking by an animal in a laboratory experiment, and then make assumptions as to its level of hunger, if food was its reward. However, the deprivation level does not relate directly to the behavioural level observed; there are multiple factors involved in behaviour – in the example quoted above, fatigue could be an influencing factor. Unless all the intervening factors can be identified, and allowed for, estimation of motivation is unlikely to be accurate or useful.

Evaluation of Models of Motivation

None of the homeostatic models of motivation are seen as adequate explanation for any but the simplest behaviour. Arousal theory is the only general theory of non-homeostatic behaviour which can be applied to non-human species, but it does not explain motivated behaviours such as sexual behaviour, parenting behaviour or aggression, notwithstanding the part played by gender and environmental influences. Instead of pursuing an eclectic approach, scientists are now taking a more focused approach, examining one specific behaviour at a time and identifying the neural, hormonal, environmental and other factors involved. When these are understood more thoroughly, it may be possible to move towards a clearer understanding of how these interact to produce what we term 'motivated behaviour'.

Whether we can ever hope for one all-encompassing theory of motivation is unlikely, given the complexity of behaviour available to many species. In fact, on investigation even the simple behaviours such as eating may well have more complex motivations than was first thought.

Self-Assessment Questions

1. Discuss some of the factors involved in motivation, in non-human species.
2. Describe a homeostatic model of motivation, and evaluate how useful this is in understanding motivation.
3. Describe the Arousal Theory of motivation and discuss whether it explains all behaviour in non-human animals.
4. Describe, with examples, how neural, hormonal and environmental factors interact with learning, to produce motivated behaviour.

BOX 2.1

Neural Factors in Motivation
(for readers who wish to look further into neural mechanisms)

Arousal

If we assume that arousal is an essential precursory state to motivation, we must look first at the Reticular Formation, in the brainstem, as the site of arousal. As early as 1949, Moruzzi and Magoun found that electrical stimulation of this area produced arousal in a sleeping cat. Subsequent studies have attempted to locate the exact mechanisms for arousal in this complex brain structure. Of some importance is a nucleus called the **locus coerulus**, which contain neurons of the noradrenergic system (these circulate the neurotransmitter noradrenalin). Aston-Jones and Bloom (1981) monitored electrical recordings from these neurons in rats, and found that activity increased in wakefulness and decreased in sleep. However, there is a lower rate of activity in these neurons during drinking or grooming, which are arousal activities, and therefore it is suggested that these neurons relate to vigilance, rather than arousal.

Decision-Making

Once aroused, the animal may be motivated in a specific direction, by either external or internal stimuli. In simple organisms such as *Pleurobranchaea*, decision-making processes can be traced to specific neurons (nerve cells); for example, the decision to feed rather than escape is mediated by specific neurones. In many animals, hormones inhibit feeding in favour of laying eggs. Motivation in animals lower down the phylogenetic scale is a process which can be located and identified physiologically, whereas in more complex animals, such as cats who have 10,000,000,000 neurons, the complexity of motivation and decision-making can only be described behaviourally, not pinpointed to specific anatomical features. Certainly hormones have been identified which influence courtship, mating, nest-building, egg-laying, but many other behaviours are not linked to hormones and cannot as yet be related to specific neurons with any certainty.

Eating and Drinking

In higher animals, osmoreceptors (for detecting fluids) and glucoreceptors (for detecting food) are distributed not only in the mouth and oesophagus, but other digestive areas and also the central nervous system. In rats, the osmoreceptors which detect thirst are located in the anterior hypothalamus and preoptic area of the brain (Peck and Blass, 1975), while the lateral hypothalamus appears to play a role in prompting eating behaviour (Winn, Tarbuck and Dunnett, 1984;

Dunnett, Lane and Winn, 1985), together with a neurotransmitter called **neuropeptide Y**, which is active in the same area. The hypothalamus has direct links with the pituitary gland which directs other glands in the body, therefore there are close hormonal/neural interchanges of information regarding motivational states. Integrated information is available to the animal from all these sources, and undoubtedly from others which scientists have not yet identified.

Sexual Behaviour

In males, the **medial preoptic area** (MPA) of the brain, just below the hypothalamus, has been shown to be critical for male sexual behaviour; destruction of this region permanently abolishes male sexual behaviour and the effects have been demonstrated in rodents, dogs, cats, goats, lizards and monkeys (Sachs and Meisel, 1988). This region has a high number of **androgen** receptors (male hormones, although also present in females in small amounts). In females, the critical area of the brain for the performance of sexual behaviour is the **ventromedial hypothalamus** (VMH). Hormones promoting sexual behaviour are esradiol followed by progesterone; receptor sites for these are present in the VMH. Males also circulate these hormones, but in lower quantiities than female and have fewer receptor sites available for them.

Maternal/Paternal Behaviour

A rise in hormonal levels of either progesterone (the principal hormone of pregnancy) or prolactin (after birth), produces nesting behaviour in rodents, suggested Voci and Carlson (1973). Oxytocin, as a hormone, stimulates milk production after birth; it also serves as a neurotransmitter, facilitating maternal behaviour.

The **medial preoptic area** (MPA), which we saw was critical for male sexual behaviour, is the critical area in females for maternal behaviour. Numan (1974) lesioned the MPA in female rats and found that while sexual behaviour was unaffected, nest building and maternal behaviours were disrupted. The MPA contains estrogen receptors; secretions of estradiol rise when the mother gives birth, and progesterone levels fall.

Aggressive Behaviour

Adams's study with rats (1986) suggested that offensive aggression is controlled by the **ventral tegmental area** of the mid-brain. Lesions here abolish offensive behaviour without affecting predation or defensive behaviour. Both predatory and defensive behaviours are mediated through the **periaqueductal grey matter** (PAG); electrical stimulation of the **ventral PAG** produced predatory behaviour in cats, while stimulation of the **dorsal PAG** produced defensive behaviour (Shaikh and Siegel, 1989).

The hypothalamus seems to control the occurrence, or frequency, of aggressive behaviours, of all three types. The **amygdala**, another structure in the limbic system of the brain, seems to be inhibitory, directly in the case of predatory behaviour; in the case of defensive behaviour the amygdala appears to inhibit aggression against another individual which has previously inflicted defeat.

Other Behaviours

More complex behaviours such as play, curiosity, self-actualisation, have not been tied to specific physiological mechanisms. The factors involved in them are too involved to be analysed at the current level of knowledge.

FURTHER READING

N. R. Carlson, *Foundations of Physiological Psychology*, 2nd edn (Needham Heights: Allyn & Bacon, 1992).

R. A. Hinde, (1966) *Animal Behaviour* (London: McGraw-Hill, 1966).

J. R. Krebs and N. B. Davies, *An Introduction to Behavioural Ecology*, 3rd edn (Oxford: Blackwell, 1993).

T. Malim, A. Birch and A. Wadeley, *Perspectives in Psychology* (Basingstoke: Macmillan, 1992).

A. Manning and M. S. Dawkins, *Animal Behaviour*, 4th edn (Cambridge: Cambridge University Press, 1992).

Don't ask me to sort it out, girl, I'm worn out! I've been pecking at lights all day just to earn us a bit of birdseed!

Learning and Behaviour 3

At the end of this chapter you should be able to:

1. Understand what is meant by learning and appreciate the distinction between laboratory-based and ethological studies of learning.
2. Discuss several different forms of simple learning including habituation, classical conditioning and operant conditioning and be aware of some of the biological limits of conditioning in animals.
3. Have explored some more-complex forms of learning observed in animals, particularly cognitive learning, including the formation of cognitive maps, insight learning and learning sets.
4. Consider evidence derived from comparative studies of learning and be aware of some problems which arise in such research.
5. Assess evidence for the phenomena of thinking and memory in animals.
6. Critically evaluate some of the clinical and educational applications of learning theory to humans.

INTRODUCTION

Psychologists have traditionally been interested in learning. During the first half of this century, a great deal of effort was directed towards the study of animal learning and two convenient species were generally used in laboratory studies, the rat and the pigeon. Much of this early work on learning was done from a behaviourist perspective (see Box 3.1) By investigating a wide range of different learning situations, it was hoped to arrive at general 'laws of learning' that might apply to most species, including humans. Many different models and theories of learning were produced. Munn (1950) provided a comprehensive record of this 'heroic age' of experimental psychology.

BOX 3.1

The Behaviourist Approach to Learning

Behaviourism shaped the course of psychology during the first half of this century. Its leading exponent, John Watson (1913), attacked the then current emphasis on studying consciousness and mental experience. He contended that psychology should be about the study of **observable behaviour** – what animals and humans actually *do*. It was not possible, he believed, to study vague processes such as consciousness and other mental states which could not be directly observed.

Watson and his colleagues believed that behaviour is moulded by experience. Thus, they had a natural interest in learning. They argued that learned behaviour in animals and humans came about through the formation of simple associations between stimuli in the environment and responses made to these stimuli by the organism (stimulus-response units). Watson's views of learning relied to a great extent on the work of Pavlov into conditioned reflexes in dogs. Following the work of Watson and his followers, behaviourism gathered strength and its principles and rigorous methods of study became an integral part of psychology. This momentum was sustained to a large extent in contemporary psychology by the efforts of another major behaviourist, B. F. Skinner. Skinner worked with animals on a form of learning known as **operant conditioning**. He later extended principles derived from his work with animals to aspects of human behaviour. (The work of both Pavlov and Skinner are discussed later in this section).

More recently, psychologists who were dissatisfied with the old laboratory-based theories of learning have drawn inspiration from ethologists, who have traditionally studied animal learning in more natural settings (Rescorla, 1988). (Refer back to Chapter 1 for a discussion of laboratory-based and ethological approaches to the study of animal behaviour.)

The rigid models of learning proposed by the behaviourists have been replaced by a much more biologically based approach. Such an approach recognises that an animal's learning abilities have evolved to accommodate its own particular needs. It is clear, too, that though there may be general laws of learning which apply to most species, there also appear to be different learning mechanisms which seem to occur in different species. Psychologists now study animal behaviour for its own sake. Nonetheless, there is a great interest in what the study of animals can tell us about human behaviour and this chapter will reflect that interest.

This chapter will focus on some accounts of learning and will attempt to explore the answers to questions such as

- What do we mean by learning?
- How does learning take place – what are the processes involved?
- What are the biological constraints on learning in animals?
- Are there learning processes which are applicable to both animals and humans?

There will be no attempt to provide a comprehensive survey of types and conditions of learning, but rather discussion of a selection of situations that have been widely studied and which are relevant to comparative psychology.

SECTION I DIFFERENT KINDS OF LEARNING

What Is Learning?

Thorpe (1963) studied learning in a wide range of different species, including insects, birds and mammals. He defined learning as '... that process which manifests itself by adaptive changes in individual behaviour as a result of experience'. It is important to note that this does not include behavioural changes which might result from disease, nor those which are due to maturation.

As we have seen in Chapter 1, generation by generation, animal species adapt to changing environmental conditions by natural selection. This adaptation involves the development of behaviours that are helpful for survival of the species. Individual members of animal species adapt to their environment by learning how to cope with the problems arising from changing conditions. An animal that finds food or a mate more effectively on a subsequent occasion than it did previously is demonstrating its ability to learn. Further, learning is seen as a way in which animals attempt to detect the most vital features of a changing environment, identifying the most consistent influences and ignoring those that are less important for them. We shall now consider some different kinds of learning starting with some of the simpler mechanisms.

Simple Learning

1. Habituation

Habituation is thought to be the very simplest form of learning necessary for survival of animals. It involves learning not to respond to a particular stimulus. Learning what not to do is as important to an animal or human as learning to respond to particular signals. By learning to ignore innocuous stimulation, the animal's energy can be conserved for other, more important activities (Thorpe, 1963) For example, birds will learn to ignore the scarecrow that previously caused them to flee; they habituate; humans may habituate to the ticking of a clock or the sound of traffic noise.

Clark (1960) demonstrated habituation in marine rag worms, Nereis, which live in tubes they have constructed in the sandy floor of the sea. In the laboratory, Clark was able to get the worms to live in glass tubes in shallow basins of water. He found that touching the protruding head of the worm, jarring the basin, a sudden shadow passing over and various other stimuli caused the worms to retract into the tube. The majority of worms re-emerged within a minute. If the stimuli were repeated every minute, the number of worms responding gradually diminished until none were retracting; they had habituated.

The phenomenon of habituation shows that animals can learn to ignore a stimulus which continues to be experienced, so conserving energy for other more necessary functions.

Habituation also forms the basis of a technique used in research when it is unclear whether or not an animal can recognise a particular stimulus. For example, Ryan (1982) investigated whether a pigeon could recognise others of the same species by first placing an object pigeon next to it and recording the frequency of the bowing fixed action pattern which occurred. After about five 5-minute trials, the subject pigeon ceased to bow – it had habituated. When a second object pigeon, identical to the first one to the human eye, was presented, the subject's bowing promptly recommenced. The method of habituation is also commonly used with human babies to study the perception of form, movement and colour (Bornstein, 1988)

2. Associative Learning

This relates to the kind of learning that takes place when a stimulus becomes associated with another stimulus or with particular consequences. For example, a baby learns to associate the sight of a feeding bottle with milk; a dog learns to 'sit' because a reward is given; in an experiment, a honey bee picks out the blue dish from a selection of dishes because it has previously found sugar solution there: it has associated sugar with the colour blue. The best known types of associative learning are classical and operant (or instrumental) conditioning.

Classical Conditioning

Reflex behaviour is involuntary; it arises automatically in response to an appropriate stimulus; examples are salivating at the smell of food, feeling fear when faced with something frightening. The theory of classical conditioning aims to account for the way in which reflex behaviour may become associated with a new stimulus that does not naturally activate that behaviour. Put simply, an individual may learn to respond in a particular way to a given stimulus because of its association with something else. **Pavlov** (1927), a physiologist, was studying the salivary reflex in dogs when he observed that the dogs salivated not only at the sight and smell of food, a 'natural' response, but also at the sight of the food container alone. Through a series of experiments, he demonstrated that dogs could be conditioned to salivate to other 'unnatural' stimuli, such as a buzzer being sounded, provided the stimulus was repeatedly presented at, or slightly before, the presentation of food. Such a pairing caused an association to be formed between the buzzer and the food and subsequently between the buzzer and the salivation response. A **conditional reflex** had been formed.

Figure 3.1 illustrates the process of classical conditioning and the terminology associated with it.

Pavlov further demonstrated that the following processes could occur after conditioning:

- If the conditional stimulus continued to be present but without the food, the salivating response would cease or become **extinguished**.

FIGURE 3.1
The Process of Classical Conditioning

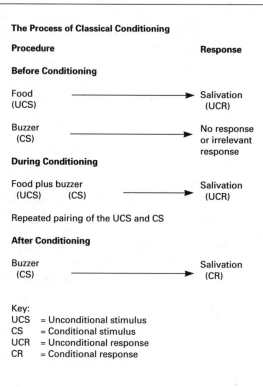

Key:
UCS = Unconditional stimulus
CS   = Conditional stimulus
UCR = Unconditional response
CR   = Conditional response

Source: Birch and Malim (1988).

- After extinction, the conditional response, salivation may reappear when the relevant stimulus is present, though it is muchweaker. This reappearance is known an **spontaneous recovery.**
- The dog would **generalise** its response by salivating to sounds similar to the buzzer.
- The opposite process to generalisation is **discrimination**: if two different tones were sounded but food was presented with only one of them, the dog would learn to discriminate between them and salivate only to the tone associated with food.

The last process, **conditioned discrimination**, has been of great value for measuring the perceptual abilities of animals. After the animal has been trained to respond to one particular stimulus, for example a certain shape, colour or sound, it can then be tested to see how far it can discriminate this stimulus from others of increasing similarity. To give two examples from many hundreds, von Frisch (1967) used this method in his classic studies of the colour vision of bees; Wells (1962) used it to investigate the sensitivity of touch in the octopus.

Conditioned reflexes of the kind investigated by Pavlov have been observed in many different animals. For example, birds learn to avoid the black and orange caterpillars of the cinnabar moth after finding that the taste of them is offensive; then they generalise this avoidance response to wasps and other black and orange patterned insects (Manning and Dawkins, 1992).

In natural settings. a 'pure' conditioned reflex is not so apparent as in a laboratory experiment. For example, foraging bees do not simply learn to associate a colour with the nectar reward, they also learn at what time during the day the nectar secretion is highest and also the location of the flowers relative to their hive.

Operant Conditioning

Unlike classical conditioning, operant, or instrumental conditioning is concerned with voluntary rather than reflex behaviour. The theory is based on Thorndike's (1913) **Law of Effect** which states that behaviour resulting in pleasant consequences is likely to be repeated in the same circumstances, whereas that which has no such pleasant consequences dies away.

Thorndike investigated this type of learning with cats using a 'puzzle box' – a cage with a door that could only be opened from inside by pulling a loop of string. Typically a cat was placed in the box and tried hard to escape. In the course of its efforts, – by chance – it pulled the string and escaped through the open door. Several more trials were carried out and eventually the cat pulled the string immediately it was placed in the box. Thorndike measured the time taken by the cat to escape as an indicator of learning. His data showed that learning the correct 'escape' behaviour happened gradually – a situation he named **trial and error learning**. The reward (freedom) he contended was responsible for 'stamping in' the appropriate response.

Operant conditioning is similar in principle to Thorndike's trial and error learning. In his book *Behaviour of Organisms* (1938), Skinner described a series of laboratory experiments he conducted with rats. He constructed a small box containing a lever, a food dispenser and (sometimes) a panel to display lighted stimuli. A rat placed in the box spontaneously explores its surroundings and eventually, by accident, presses the lever. This activates the food dispenser and a pellet of food is presented to the rat. Subsequently, each time the animal's behaviour approximates to what is required, food is presented until eventually the 'reward' known as **reinforcement** is produced only when the animal presses the lever. This procedure is known as **behaviour shaping**; the desired behaviour is shaped by rewarding a series of responses that are **successive approximations** – that is, they approximate more and more closely to the desirable behaviour. The desirable behaviour, in this case, lever pressing – was named an operant. The reward, which increases the likelihood of the behaviour (or operant) being repeated, is the **reinforcer**. The process whereby the food is presented in response to the lever-pressing behaviour is known as **positive reinforcement**.

Skinner and others have repeatedly demonstrated that the techniques of operant conditioning can be used to produce quite complex behaviour in animals. By carefully shaping the component behaviours, he trained pigeons to act as pilots in rockets and to play table tennis.

As with classical conditioning, generalisation, discrimination and extinction can be demonstrated:

- An animal may **generalise** its response to situations which are similar but not identical to the one in which it was originally conditioned. Therefore, if a rat is conditioned to respond when a one-inch plastic square is presented, it will also press the lever in response to a circle of a similar size.
- A rat may be conditioned to discriminate between the circle and the square if it is reinforced only when it presses the bar in response to one of them, but not the other.
- If reinforcement is discontinued, **extinction** of the operant response will occur. For reasons which are not clear, this takes longer than with classical conditioning.

Schedules of Reinforcement   Skinner also demonstrated that the kind of patterns, or schedules, of reinforcement given would differentially affect the kind of learning which occurred. The two main schedules are

● **Continuous reinforcement** – when a reward is given to every instance of the desired behaviour.
● **Partial reinforcement** – where an animal is reinforced only some of the time.

The four partial reinforcement schedules that are most commonly used are:

1. **Fixed interval**: the animal is reinforced after regular time intervals, say every 50 seconds, provided at least one lever-pressing response is made during that time.
2. **Variable interval:** reinforcement is given *on average* every, say, 50 seconds, though not precisely at the same time intervals.
3. **Fixed ratio**: the animal is reinforced after a regular number of lever-pressing responses, say after every four responses.
4. **Variable ratio**: reinforcement is given *on average* every, say, four responses, though not exactly after each fourth response.

Each schedule has a different effect on learning. In general, continuous reinforcement produces the quickest learning, while partial reinforcement produces learning which lasts longer in the absence of reinforcement.

The Consequences of Behaviour Skinner believed that behaviour is shaped by its consequences. We have already noted that one such consequence is positive reinforcement, something which is pleasant. Other consequences might be **negative reinforcement** and **punishment.**

Negative reinforcement refers to the removal or avoidance of something unpleasant. For example, an electric shock is switched off when the rat presses the lever. This is known as **escape learning**. Skinner showed also that if a light is flashed just before an electric shock is given, the rat would learn to press the lever in response to the light, thus avoiding the shock – an example of **avoidance learning**. Like positive reinforcement, negative reinforcement results in the desired behaviour being **strengthened**.

Punishment refers to the delivery of an undesirable stimulus following a response, for example, when an electric shock is given in response to the lever-pressing behaviour. Skinner believed that just as reinforcement (positive and negative) can be used to strengthen a response, making it more likely to be repeated, so punishment *weakens* the response and makes it less likely to recur. However, he argued that punishment is not a suitable technique for controlling behaviour, since it simply suppresses unwanted behaviour without strengthening desirable behaviour. Studies with rats carried out by Estes (1944, 1970) showed that punishment appeared only to diminish lever-pressing behaviour for a short time, but did not weaken it in the long term.

A cautionary note so far as children are concerned is that 'punishment' for bad behaviour could well be reinforcing, if the reason for the behaviour is attention-seeking. Any attention – even smacking – may be better than none.

Secondary Reinforcement   Some stimuli, known as **secondary reinforcers**, become reinforcing because they are associated with primary reinforcers such as food or water. Thus, Skinner found that a rat would press the lever in response to the clicking noise heard when a food pellet was delivered, even on occasions when no food was in fact produced.

The conventional view of operant conditioning was that reinforcement is only effective if it is given quickly following a response such as bar-pressing – a principle known as **contiguity**. The principle of secondary reinforcement has proved useful in overcoming the adverse effects of delayed reward. For example, secondary reinforcers such as clicking noises are useful for training animals, as in a circus when it would be difficult to give a reward immediately after the animal's response.

Biological Limits of Conditioning

The descriptions of classical and operant conditioning above suggest that the two learning processes are quite straightforward – animals learn to associate a stimulus with a reinforcement (classical conditioning) or a response with a reinforcement (operant conditioning). However, in practice, if one brings an ethological approach into laboratory situations, it is clear that animals often bring their own natural species-specific behaviours to a learning situation and these may affect the way they respond. An interesting example comes from pigeons used in operant conditioning studies because they will readily learn to peck at a key on the wall of the Skinner box to obtain a reward of either food or water. Close examination of the pigeon's pecking behaviour shows that when hungry and pecking for a food reward, the pigeon's bill is open and its eyes are partially closed. However, when pecking for water the bill is almost closed and the eyes are fully open (see Figure 3.2).

These two 'styles' of pecking mirror exactly the contrasting styles used in a natural setting by a pigeon pecking to pick up food grains compared to that of a pigeon which dips its bill into water to drink. In other words, the pigeon pecking in a Skinner box is treating the same key as if it were food in one situation and as water in the other.

Many other studies have shown that animals appear to learn most easily those responses which are closest to their natural behaviour and these responses may not necessarily fit with the 'general laws of learning' proposed by traditional learning theorists. For example, Breland and Breland (1961), pupils of Skinner, used techniques of operant conditioning to train animals to perform eyecatching tricks for TV commercials. They reported, however, that sometimes, instead of performing the desired behaviour, the animal would 'misbehave' and do something that was closer to its natural behaviour. So, a pig trained to drop money into a piggy bank would root with its snout on the way to the bank and chickens required to ring bells would scratch and peck at the ground instead. The Brelands came to accept that an animal does not always simply associate stimulus and response – its instinctual behaviour may set limits on what can be learned.

An example taken from an ethological perspective investigates contiguity (the need to give reinforcement at or very soon after the presentation of a stimulus or response) Barnett (1963) showed that contiguity, as demonstrated in traditional learning theory experiments, is not always necessary to ensure that learning in the form of classical conditioning takes place. He described how rats only nibble at very small amounts of any new foods that are found in their territory. If the food is subsequently found to be 'safe', they gradually eat more on successive occasions until they are eating normal amounts. If it is poisonous and they survive, they avoid it completely in future – a conditioned response. This behaviour explains why poisoning rats is no easy task. The interesting point to note from a learning theory

FIGURE 3.2

**Trained Pigeons in a Skinner Box
(from Moore, 1973)**

(a)   (b)

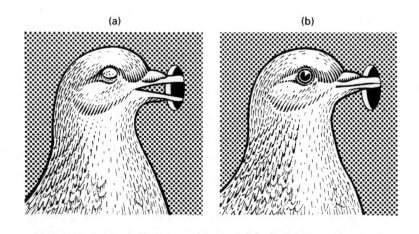

Trained pigeons in a Skinner box pecking a key to obtain a reward. In (a) the reward is food; the eyes are almost closed and the bill is opened as if to seize a food item. In (b) the bird is pecking for a water reward and the bill is almost closed whilst the eyes remain fully open.

view is that a delay of hours usually occurs between a rat tasting the poisonous bait – the conditional stimulus (always disguised with sweet substances) – and the resulting feelings of sickness – the unconditional stimulus. These findings have been confirmed also in laboratory experiments.

Further, it has been shown that while rats can learn to associate taste with sickness after one tasting and a long delay, birds are more likely to associate the *appearance* of food with the effects of sickness (Martin and Lett, 1985). Unlike rats and some other mammals, birds are visual hunters. In this way they can learn to avoid harmful foods such as poisonous caterpillars in the wild. These are very good examples of two different species learning the same thing – which foods cause sickness – by different means which fit with their natural way of selecting food.

More Complex Learning

As we have seen, classical and operant conditioning arise from an animal making associations between stimuli or events; much animal learning can be explained by reference to these two processes. However, since the early part of this century, psychologists have studied more complex forms of learning which often involve some kind of **cognitive** activity (thinking, interpreting, understanding) rather than merely making simple associations. Three examples of cognitive learning in animals will be examined: the formation of cognitive maps, insight learning and the phenomenon of learning sets.

1. Cognitive Maps

Much research has been concerned with how rats learn to negotiate their way through a complex maze. Hull (1943) envisaged the rat building up a chain of stimulus-response (S-R) associations as it moved through the maze. The rat associates a corner or turn with the goal. As it proceeds further, it learns that a previous turn leads to the first S-R association. Gradually, the maze is learned through a set of simple associations, one leading automatically to the next. Tolman (1932), however, believed that during the exploration phase, rats do not simply learn a number of right and left turning responses, but form some kind of mental picture of the whole maze – a **cognitive map**. They can then use this to find their way through, avoiding turns which may lead to a blind alley and choosing routes which lead most quickly to the goal box.

In a typical experiment, Tolman used two groups of rats – an experimental group, which were allowed to explore a maze like the one in Figure 3.3 and a control group which had no opportunity to explore the maze. Neither group was given any reinforcers such as food. Then both the experimental and control rats were placed in the maze and food was introduced as a reinforcer. Tolman found that the experimental group learned to run the maze much more quickly than the control group. He believed that this was because they had learned the layout of the maze and formed a cognitive map during their earlier, unreinforced explorations. Learning such as this which occurs without reinforcement and which can be inferred from the animal's behaviour is known as **latent learning**. The cognitive map thus enabled the rat to learn a specific route more easily once reinforcement was given.

FIGURE 3.3

A Sketch of One of Tolman's (1932) Mazes

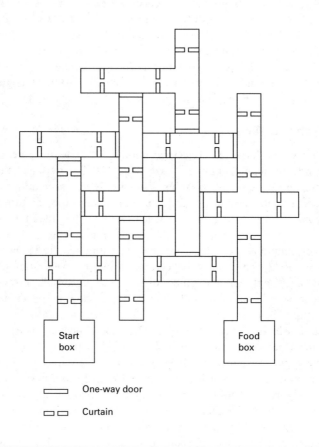

More recent research provides evidence of cognitive maps in animals. Olton (1979) carried out a study in which rats learned a maze which consisted of a centre platform with eight identical passageways radiating from it, each with food placed at the far end. The rat had to learn to visit each passageway, retrieving the food there, without visiting any one twice. The rats succeeded in this task very well. After around twenty trials, they rarely returned to a passage-way they had already visited. Interestingly, the rats visited the pass-ageways randomly rather than in an obvious order such as clockwise, suggesting that they had not learned a rigid sequence of responses. The researchers concluded that a rat developed a cognitive map of the maze which allowed it to note and recall the passageways it had already visited.

It is clear from the above studies that some animal learning in-volves quite complex cognitive activity, rather than merely the forming of S-R associations.

2. Insight Learning

Everyone has experienced the situation where after pondering a prob-lem for several minutes, the answer has 'come in a flash'. Animal researchers have argued that there are many instances of the same phenomenon in animals. They have used the term **insight learning** when they have observed animals solving problems very quickly without any obvious trial and error activities.

In an important series of experiments carried out in the 1920s, Köhler demonstrated insight learning in chimpanzees. The animals were set a series of problems to solve. In one famous example, Sultan, Köhler's most intelligent chimpanzee, was placed in a cage with a piece of fruit just out of reach (see Figure 3.4). Outside the cage were a number of sticks which if slotted together were long enough to reach the fruit. After a period of inactivity, the animal quite suddenly solved the problem by slotting the sticks together and reaching for the food. Köhler called this process 'insightful learn-ing'. He believed that during the initial period of inactivity, the animal was thinking – he called this **cognitive restructuring**. This resulted in a sudden insight into the problem followed by the ani-mal performing a solution.

There are important differences in the behaviour of Köhler's chim-panzees compared to Thorndike's cats or Skinner's rats and pigeons described in the last section:

- In the former, the solution came suddenly rather than after a period of trial and error (though it is possible that the chimpan-zees engaged in *mental* trial and error).
- Also, once the problem had been solved, the chimpanzee would

FIGURE 3.4

A Problem Situation Used by Köhler (1925) with Chimpanzees

The chimpanzee slots together two short sticks in order to reach the banana, or pulls in a longer stick which will reach the fruit.

make few irrelevant movements, unlike the Skinnerian rat which would continue to make irrelevant moves for many trials.

- Köhler's chimpanzees demonstrated that they could transfer what they had learned to a new and different situation; for example, in one situation, Sultan would pile up boxes in order to reach a bunch of bananas which were otherwise out of reach, or would fit two sticks together to pull down the bananas.

Critics have pointed out that there were methodological flaws in Köhler's work. For example, he did not always record what relevant experiences the chimpanzees had prior to the study. Also, because of a lack of strict control, his results were sometimes open to alternative interpretations. Nonetheless, his research findings have generally been accepted as valid by many psychologists and animal researchers.

3. Learning Sets

Harlow (1949) argued that insight learning as investigated by Köhler may not be a different process from operant conditioning, but merely arises from prior experience with trial and error learning. He proposed that insight learning could appear to occur if the animal formed a **learning set**. If an animal can form a learning set, it means that it has learned not just a problem, but something of the *principle* behind the problem.

In typical experiments, Harlow gave rhesus monkeys a range of discrimination tasks. For example, the monkey is presented with two dissimilar objects, say a tennis ball and a matchbox – the matchbox always covers a small item of food; the tennis ball never has a reward. After several trials, the monkey chooses the matchbox immediately. The trials are continued in the same way but using different objects. The objects are repeatedly changed after each correct discrimination. As the number of discriminations increases, the monkey learns each new task more quickly, eventually after only one trial; this is despite the fact that viewed as an individual problem, it is just as difficult as the first one. It has learned the principle behind the problem, or in Harlow's terms, has formed a learning set.

In more complex tasks, Harlow demonstrated that monkeys could learn principles such as 'odd one out' of three objects and choosing the 'left hand object' or 'plastic shape with corners such as a square or triangle.

Harlow argued that his research showed that what Köhler called 'insight learning' arose from operant conditioning which involves trial and error learning. However, it is clear that the formation of learning sets involves more than simple stimulus-response learning. In the learning-set experiments, the fact that the animals were able to learn principles such as 'odd one out' meant that at the very least, they were recalling what happened in earlier trials and then applying it in later ones. This strongly suggests that some cognitive activity occurred, since memory was involved.

Another way in which monkeys showed themselves capable of forming learning sets was in 'repeated reversal' problems. Here, the animal is trained to choose object A in preference to object B. Once learned, object B is now rewarded and object A is not; when this reversal is learned, the reward is then switched back to object A and so on. The monkeys became increasingly faster at learning each reversal, again implying that they had learned a principle.

Self-Assessment Questions

1. What do you understand by 'learning'? Explain the role played by adaptation in animal learning.
2. Explain with an example the process of habituation.
3. Briefly outline the chief features of (a) classical conditioning and (b) operant conditioning.
4. Referring to appropriate studies, discuss some of the biological limits of conditioning in animals.
5. Discuss two forms of learning in animals which seem to involve some kind of cognitive activity: for example, the acquisition of cognitive maps; learning sets; insight learning.

SECTION II   COMPARATIVE STUDY OF LEARNING AND MEMORY

As we noted at the beginning of this chapter, comparative psychology has a long history. Initially, a wide range of animals was investigated even though studies of the rat and pigeon became by far the most common. Psychologists have always been interested in the study of learning and recently those with an ethological interest have started to investigate differences in learning ability between species. Thus, there is a reasonable amount of data which may provide evidence of evolutionary changes.

This section will examine some of the evidence from comparative studies of learning along with some of the problems encountered, will explore the question of whether animals can think and will consider some research which has investigated memory mechanisms in animals.

Problems in Comparative Research

Manning and Dawkins (1992) draw attention to the following pitfalls in comparative research:

1. Our essential vanity about human intellectual ability invariably leads us to search for an upward progression among animals with human beings placed firmly at the top of the hierarchy. This has sometimes led to a failure to consider that there may be a number of poss-

ible hierarchies, each of which uses a different set of criteria. The question arises: should honey bees be judged by the same criteria as monkeys?

2. In the past, there has been an over-emphasis on laboratory studies of learning, with less effort being made to investigate the role that various kinds of learning play in the natural life of different animals.

3. Different animal groups vary widely in their sensory capacities and manipulative ability. It is therefore not easy to devise truly comparable situations for testing different animals. For example, the procedures necessary to measure discriminative conditioning in an octopus, a honey-bee and a rat need to be very different and it is not always possible to be sure that problems set are of equal difficulty or that the animals perceive them in the same way.

4. Motivation and reinforcement also present problems. The level of motivation often influences the rate of learning and may even determine whether in fact the animal learns at all. (Note that the issue of motivation in animals has been discussed in Chapter 2.) How is it possible to compare levels of hunger motivation in a rat, which can live for weeks with no food, with a fish which can survive for only a few days? Also, finding a suitable reinforcer for a particular species is difficult. A small piece of food may be an excellent reinforcer for a hungry mammal but mean little to a fish and even less to a worm. Some studies, however, have provided evidence of reinforcers which are relevant to the animals being tested. For example, Maier and Schneirla (1935) and Vowles (1965) both found that the best reinforcer for maze learning by ants was to arrive back at their nest. Escape into a darkened area seems to be best for many small invertebrates.

Because of the difficulties outlined above, some researchers have questioned the validity of any comparisons at all of intellectual ability between different animals (Macphail, 1987) However, others have attempted to devise valid comparative tests and some of the evidence collected is noted in the following sub-section.

Evidence from Comparative Studies

1. Comparisons of Brain Development

Many studies have sought to examine the correlation between brain development and learning in animals. The main question considered is whether there is a link between the structure of the brain and the degree of complexity in the animals' behaviour. The factors which have been considered include brain size and the growth of the cerebral cortex.

Brain Size   The prevalence of learning, the capacity to process information and the general complexity of behaviour are greater in mammals and birds than in fish and reptiles. These differences are thought to be linked to the evolution of a large brain – or **encephalisation** (Jerison, 1985). However, brain size is not the only important factor: whales and elephants have larger brains than humans but less learning capacity.

Growth of the Cerebral Cortex   In vertebrates, the upper part of the brain, the cerebrum, is divided into two symmetrical cerebral hemispheres, linked together with a series of fibres at the corpus callosum. The outer covering of the hemispheres, known as the **cortex**, is a sheet of nerve cells arranged in layers. It is in the cortex that 'higher mental functions' such as thinking, reasoning and problem-solving are thought to occur. The amount of cerebral cortex relative to the rest of the brain varies in different animal groups, with humans possessing the greatest amount. However, there is no simple link between the cerebral cortex and learning ability. For instance, birds have been underestimated in the past because the cortex is small relative to the size of their brains. In fact their learning ability has been found to be second only to that of the primates (see the account in Chapter 4 of the capacities of a grey parrot by Pepperberg, 1990). Birds have evolved along a separate line to that of mammals for over 200 million years and they have developed a different type of brain structure.

It is clear that brain structure alone is not a sufficient guide to learning abilities. Comparative studies of the behaviour of animals have added more to our understanding.

2. Behavioural Tests

Simple Learning Capacity There is no reliable evidence that speed of learning in simple behavioural tests varies between vertebrates or between them and invertebrates. However, there is evidence that *what* is learned does systematically vary. Gellerman (1933) described a series of experiments in which two chimpanzees and two 2-year-old children were learning that a food reward was associated with a white triangle on a black square and not with a plain black square. One child learned in a single trial but the other took 200 trials and both chimpanzees took over 800. Most rats took 20–60 trials. However, though the chimpanzee might take longer than the rat to learn this simple discrimination task, it learnt *more* about 'triangularity'.

Trained to respond to the top shape in Figure 3.5, a rat makes random responses to any of the lower figures. A chimpanzee responds to (a) and (b) but makes random responses only to (c). A two-year-old child recognises a 'triangle' in all three lower figures (Hebb, 1958).

Learning Sets It was once assumed that only more advanced mammals were capable of forming learning sets (see p. 92). However, in a review of comparative studies, Warren (1965) suggested that all vertebrates with the exception of fish could do so. In more recent research, Mackintosh *et al.* (1985) showed that goldfish can form repeated reversal sets such as those described on page 93, as can the octopus.

The speed with which learning sets are acquired differs dramatically between different animal groups. For example, Mackintosh (1983) compared rats and goldfish in a simple reversal experiment. Both learned the original reversal with roughly the same number of errors, suggesting that both animals found the problem of equal difficulty. However, afterwards, rats improved much more quickly than goldfish. In more difficult discrimination tasks, rats performed more slowly than dogs, cats or primates. No study has demonstrated that fish can ever improve their speed of learning in this situation.

Conclusions on Comparative Studies of Learning

Manning and Dawkins (1992) suggest that we can cautiously conclude that cats and dogs show more signs of 'intelligence' than rodents and that primates do show greater superiority. However, they point

FIGURE 3.5

The Concept of Triangularity (from Hebb, 1958)

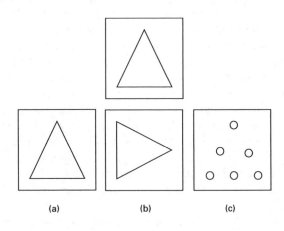

(a)   (b)   (c)

out that many learning experiments do not do justice to the enormous flexibility and ingenuity of animals such as chimpanzees. Also, we may be influenced by their similarity to ourselves, especially as they can manipulate objects in the same way as we do.

It is possible that we underestimate the intelligence of other animals because they do not have good hands and good eyesight. Because their structure and environment is so different from our own, it is only recently that we have become aware of the exceptional intelligence of dolphins.

Can Animals Think?

No-one who has kept a pet or who has observed animals closely in the wild can have failed to wonder whether they 'think', 'reflect' on their actions or have a 'mind' and 'consciousness. These words are in inverted commas because though we are all aware that these phenomena exist in ourselves, it is quite difficult to define them precisely; it is even more difficult to find evidence that they exist in animals. The information about these issues tends to be unsystematic and often anecdotal. Nonetheless, it is of considerable interest to many comparative psychologists.

Before discussing the question of whether animals have higher mental processes, it is important to be aware of some of the errors which can occur when interpreting animal behaviour.

Lloyd Morgan's Canon and Anthropomorphism

A principle which has generally guided comparative psychologists in their work with animals is known as **Lloyd Morgan's Canon**. Early this century, Lloyd Morgan, one of the pioneers of comparative psychology, proposed that animal behaviour should not be interpreted as arising from higher mental processes if it could be interpreted in terms of simpler mechanisms. Morgan's guiding principle has enabled comparative psychologists to avoid some of the more absurd explanations of animal behaviour proposed in the past. Two examples of such explanations are relevant.

- Around the turn of the century in Germany, Baron von Osten claimed that his horse (nicknamed 'Clever Hans') could actually count and calculate sums. On being presented with a sum, for example 5 + 6, the horse would give an answer by beating the ground with its hoof the correct number of times. It transpired that the horse was simply responding to unconscious changes in its owner's facial expression when it arrived at the correct answer.
- Around the same time, Lewis Morgan (not to be confused with Lloyd Morgan) claimed that beavers possessed a complex understanding of hydraulics which enabled them to construct dams and channels.

These two, clearly absurd, claims about the thought processes of animals are classic examples of **anthropomorphism** – the tendency to attribute to animals human characteristics for which there is no real evidence.

Comparative psychologists generally work hard to develop objective techniques for studying animal behaviour and to avoid anthropomorphism in their interpretations. However, in doing so, researchers may fail to recognise that some animals might well be capable of thinking, reflecting and planning.

Animal Thinking or Anthropomorphism?

Manning and Dawkins (1992) describe three examples of animal behaviour which may indicate true 'thinking'.

1. **'Insight' in an orang-utan**: Alfred Russell Wallace, the famous biologist who collaborated with Charles Darwin in his original theory of evolution, made some observations at the end of the last century. Whilst visiting the island of Borneo, Wallace studied a captive orang-utan. Close to the cage, a number of domestic chickens foraged for food. The orang repeatedly attempted to catch one, but they always managed to escape. On one occasion, Wallace saw the orang scatter grain from its food dish outside the cage, scattering some seed very close to the bars. It then sat quietly as the chickens discovered the grain and pecked their way right up to the cage. In a flash, the orang shot out its arm, caught one of the birds and killed it. (Compare this to Köhler's example of the ape, Sultan, on page 91.)

2. **'Problem-solving' in a sheep-dog**: Vines (1981) describes how a sheep-dog dealt with the problem of a stubborn ewe, which refused to join the main flock. After a number of unsuccessful encounters with the ewe, the dog returned to the main flock, cut off several sheep and shepherded them over to the stubborn ewe. The ewe immediately joined this group, whereupon the dog shepherded them all back to the main flock.

3. **'Anticipation' in honey-bees**: A number of people have recorded, rather than studied, some interesting behaviour in honey-bees. Honey-bees are known to communicate with each other about the nature and location of food by performing an intricate 'dance' system. (See Chapter 4 for a detailed account of this form of communication.) When studying communication in honey-bees, it is often necessary to train them to forage at a dish several metres from the hive. For example, in one study described in Chapter 4, Esch *et al.* (1965) found variations in the speed of the dance depending upon how far from the hive the food was placed. Typically, in such studies, a dish of sugar solution is colour-marked and placed on the board of the hive. Once the bees start to feed, the dish is moved further out and then further. Initially, moves of more than a metre or two causes

some difficulty, but as the day passes it is possible to move the dish 20 metres or more. At this point, researchers have reported an extraordinary occurrence. Often, as they move the dish to a new position, they find bees already there flying around looking for the food. Colour markings show that these are not newcomers attracted by the 'dance' and searching haphazardly in the same general direction; they are the original bees 'anticipating' the next position of the food source.

Manning and Dawkins have made a number of interesting observations about the above examples, whilst bearing in mind that they are 'one-off' situations which makes generalisation difficult:

1. The descriptions of the orang-utan and the sheep-dog are isolated cases; the behaviour observed may not be seen again. However, this does not make them any less interesting or important. Some animal observers will argue that to have observed such behaviour at all significantly enlightens our view of animals. Others are more cautious: perhaps the orang spilt its food accidentally; Wallace's belief that he had witnessed true insight could be misguided. A question mark is thus raised both over the accuracy of the observations and over their interpretations.
2. Similar comments could be applied to the behaviour of the sheep-dog. Dogs often have trouble with individual sheep. Nothing was known about the past experiences of this dog and it might simply have imitated the behaviour of older dogs during its training.
3. The example of the honey-bees is extraordinary because the behaviour came from an insect. We are usually reluctant to consider the possibility that insects might think about the future or work out that a food dish may next appear in a particular location. However, this may well be the correct explanation. It is as well to note, though, that in the paragraphs which follow, an alternative explanation is proposed.

Griffin's study of animal thinking: Griffin (1984) in an important book entitled *Animal Thinking* argued that although animal behaviour is not easy to interpret, it must now be accepted that true thought processes and some kind of consciousness must exist in some mammals and birds. From an evolutionary perspective, it is hard to accept that mind and consciousness in human beings have not arisen from similar processes in those animals from whom we have descended. However, even if this argument is accepted, we should not accept that honey-bees have such capabilities without attempting first to eliminate other possible explanations.

In attempting to interpret the behaviour of the honey-bees cited above, Griffin suggests that there might be a simple explanation. In their normal lives, honey-bees sometimes follow a food supply which extends out in one direction. This occurs when the sun rises and the shadow of a hill or trees moves gradually off a flower crop; the flowers begin to open and emit nectar as they are warmed by the sun. This allows the bees to extend their feeding range as the shadow moves. It might follow from this, that the ability to move out along a line of food dishes may be a function of some inborn ability. Some kind of automatic and unconscious 'rule' might be operating as it appears to in the bees' amazing dance communication referred to earlier.

A Theory of Mind

As was noted in the previous sub-section, it is possible that an unconscious and automatic 'rule' might operate to affect behaviour in some animals. However, such a proposition is not sufficient to explain the behaviour of others. For example, Premack and Woodruff (1978) carried out a series of experiments which were designed to investigate thought processes in chimpanzees. A major aim was to try to discover whether the animals were capable of recognising that individuals other than themselves had thought processes which are similar to their own. Such an understanding has become known as a **theory of mind**. If it were shown that animals do possess a theory of mind, it could be assumed that they should be capable of inferring wants, beliefs and intentions in others.

In one study, the researchers set up a situation where a chimpanzee was shown video pictures of a human being who clearly had a need for something. For example, one picture portrayed the person as huddled and shivering with cold in a room which had an unlit heater; another revealed the person vainly trying to open a locked door. The chimpanzee was then shown pictures of a series of objects (familiar to the animal), each of which could provide a remedy for the situation shown in the video, for example a burning wick for the heater; a key for the door. The researchers reasoned that to select the right picture, the animal would need to

(a) anticipate the need of the person as distinct from itself, and
(b) choose a solution as it might do so for itself.

In fact, the chimpanzees appeared to be capable of performing these mental operations. One chimpanzee chose the 'correct' picture seven times out of eight. Premack and Woodruff claimed that their experiments demonstrated that chimpanzees do possess a theory of mind.

The research provoked a lively debate about the existence of a theory of mind in animals. Astington *et al.* (1988) drew attention to the views of one participant in the debate, Dennett (1978). Dennett was not convinced that Premack and Woodruff's research methods had succeeded in demonstrating that chimpanzees possess a theory of mind and made the following observations (as quoted in Astington *et al.*, 1988):

the spirit of Dennett's list of minimal requirements is simply that

• one should refrain from attributing a theory of mind to any organism whose own way of going about things can be just as easily understood without such mentalistic assumptions; and
• any candidate who is suspected of having such a theory of mind but cannot openly persuade us of this fact in his or her own words, must be set some behavioral task that makes the having or not having of such a theory explicit.

(Astington *et al.*, 1988, pp. 393–4)

Clearly, Dennett did not believe that Premack and Woodruff's research had fulfilled these requirements.

It is important to note that Premack and Woodruff's original research report and the debate which followed stimulated a flurry of research into children's understanding of the minds of others. Such research has gathered momentum and theory of mind is currently a major focus in developmental psychology (the study of how humans develop and change over time). However, this is beyond the scope of the current book.

The Study of Memory

Learning could not occur without memory. To learn, it must be possible to store the results of experience and recall them to advantage later. As with learning itself, comparative research has been carried out into memory mechanisms. Important evidence has been collected from certain molluscs, the honey-bee and some mammals. The study of human memory has provided many rich insights. Unlike animals, humans can report what they can and cannot remember, though their recollections are not always dependable. (See Malim, 1994 for a detailed account of the study of human memory.)

Manning and Dawkins (1992) have argued that the study of memory clearly must include an investigation of the neurophysiological and biochemical aspects of how the nervous system can store some kind of representation of past experiences, in some cases for a lifetime. Despite much research, how memories of events are stored in the nervous system is still a matter of some speculation.

Two possible explanations of how the nervous system records memories of events are

1. The nervous system works by the transmission of electrical activity in neurons (nerve cells) along defined pathways. It is likely that the process of learning causes increased activity in those pathways which record stimulation of the sense organs. However, it does not seem likely that increased activity *per se* could constitute memory and that a memory could be recorded in the form of continuous flows of neural impulses moving around the same pathways for long periods of time.
2. A more likely explanation is that when a memory is formed, some kind of structural change occurs in the nervous system so that some channels are made more accessible. It is now generally thought that this is the case. This explanation suggests that memory storage must be represented in a physical form.

Whilst accepting that one should investigate the biological basis of memory, Manning and Dawkins (1992) argue that the most important evidence for memory must be found by observing behaviour. What an animal does shows what it has learnt, stored and then recalled; from these observations it is then possible to infer memory mechanisms and then check them physiologically and biochemically.

Different Kinds of Memory

It is well established that not all our experiences are stored in the same way in memory. We can look up a page number in the index of a book and then find it impossible to remember it five minutes later; on the other hand, we can recall the addresses of friends even after many years. It has been suggested that the former is an example of **short-term memory** and the latter of **long-term memory**.

Evidence for the existence of these two different memory stores comes from many sources. One source which is relevant to the study of memory in animals takes account of clinical studies of amnesia. People who have sustained a head injury or a severe shock are often unable to recall events that preceded the injury, though their short-term memory may be intact. This phenomenon is known as **retrograde amnesia**. Interestingly, where recovery occurs, the most distant memories tend to return before the recent ones. The condition of retrograde amnesia can also be created in animals. This is demonstrated in studies carried out by Andrew (1985) which are described below.

Manning and Dawkins have suggested that the process by which events are transferred to long-term memory is more labile and sensitive to disturbance than the store itself. Support for this conclusion comes also from studies with rats and chicks using drugs which affect the functioning of the nervous system. For example, low doses of strychnine or pecrotoxin which are powerful stimulants can actually enhance the early stages of memory if they are administered just before or just after a new task is learned. However, if a drug which blocks protein synthesis – for example, puromycin – is given at the same stage, memory of the new task does not consolidate and fades rapidly, though long-term memories are not affected (Andrew, 1991; McGaugh, 1989).

In studies using these techniques, the animal is presented with a task which can be recalled accurately after a single trial. For example, a chick learns not to peck at a coloured bead after finding on just one occasion that the bead is coated with a very bitter substance. In a study using the kind of task described, Andrew (1985) showed the following:

1. There are drugs which affect memory specifically at each of three time phases: short term, intermediate term and long term. They are ineffective if used earlier or later (see Figure 3.6).

FIGURE 3.6

A Scheme for the Three Stages of Memory Storage Proposed by Andrew (1985)

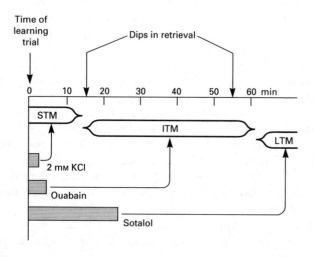

Source: Manning and Dawkins (1992) (modified from Andrew, 1985).

Andrew suggested that this indicated three types of memory which he called **short term**, **intermediate term** and **long term**.

2. Corresponding to these periods of drug sensitivity, the ability to recall fluctuates precisely. Figure 3.6 shows these fluctuations. First, chickens pecked at a coloured bead coated with a bitter substance. Then, different batches of chickens were tested for their reaction to the beads. Initially recall was good; they avoided beads similar to the bitter one. After 14–15 minutes, however, memory faded. This was not normal 'forgetting' because recall returned a minute or so later. Fifty-five minutes after the initial event, a second dip in recall occurred. Finally, memory recovered more permanently.

Similar studies with rats also showed two dips in recall before long-term memory was established, although the timing was slightly different. There were parallel findings too with honey-bees; their recall fell sharply after a learning experience and then recovered to a sustained level by ten minutes (Erber, 1981).

Manning and Dawkins believe that the studies described show the following:

1. The precise timing of their ability to recall events suggests that animals retrieve their memories from different stores in turn. A dip in recall seems to result from the process of moving from a store that is fading to the next one which is forming.
2. The nature of these processes remains to be investigated as does an explanation of how the different phases of memory interact with each other. Does each phase play a part in the formation of the next phase or does each form and fade concurrently, possibly interacting and conveying information as it fades and the next phase develops?
3. However they interact, each phase must contain a representation of what has been learned. Long-term memory is shown to be formed in around an hour. As mentioned earlier the formation of long-term memory probably results in changes in the structure of the brain which create neural impulses along new pathways. The processes involved in establishing short-term and intermediate memory probably involve nervous activity alone. This could explain why they eventually fade and why they are susceptible to physical shock and to drugs.

The study of memory is an exciting and relatively new area of research in comparative psychology. Studies by Mishkin and Appenzeller (1987) have further investigated the three phases of memory referred to above (Mishkin and Appenzeller, 1987). Other research has considered the nature of long-term memory. Horn (1985, 1990) has reviewed the work of Bateson, Horn, Rose and colleagues, who studied imprinting by newly hatched chicks as a learning and memory system.

Self-Assessment Questions

1. Discuss some of the problems encountered when comparative research is carried out.
2. Evaluate some of the evidence drawn from attempts to compare intellectual ability between different animal species.

3. How would you respond to the question 'Can animals think'?
4. Briefly outline two likely explanations of how the nervous system may record memories.
5. Discuss some research which has provided evidence of three stages of memory storage in animals.

SECTION III   APPLICATIONS OF LEARNING THEORY TO HUMANS

So far, the main thrust of this chapter has been towards learning processes as they have been observed in animals, though some comparisons have been made with human learning. The current section aims to focus on some ways in which particular theories of learning, developed using animals, have been deliberately applied to practical situations involving humans. The following three areas will be considered:

1. **Behavioural therapies** which aim to remove maladaptive (inappropriate) behaviours and substitute desirable ones, drawing on the theories of **classical and operant conditioning** (see Section I).
2. **Biofeedback** techniques, which employ the theoretical bases of both **classical and operant conditioning** in clinical settings.
3. **Programmed learning**, a method of instruction which applies the principles of **operant conditioning** to formal learning situations in educational fields.

1. Behavioural Therapies

Therapeutic techniques based on conditioning processes are usually referred to as either **behaviour modification** or **behaviour therapy**. All the techniques to be discussed assume that maladaptive responses, for example obsessive-compulsive behaviour, are the result of faulty learning and can be remedied through new learning. Walker (1984) proposed that techniques based on operant conditioning should be referred to as behaviour modification and techniques which rely upon the principles of classical conditioning should be known as behaviour therapy. This distinction is used in the sub-sections which follow.

Behaviour Modification

This is a technique which is used to change or remove unwanted behaviour. Its central principle, taken from operant conditioning, is that behaviour which is **positively reinforced** is likely to be repeated and behaviour which is ignored is likely to die out (see Thorndike's Law of Effect on page **83**). The desired behaviour is broken down into a sequence of small steps. Each step achieved is immediately rewarded, but gradually more and more of the required behaviour is demanded before the reward is given (compare the description on page **84** of **behaviour shaping through successive approximations**).

A range of childhood problems are dealt with by operant techniques, for example, bedwetting, thumb sucking, hyperactivity, poor school performance, extreme social withdrawal. Young children are under the control of adults, and therefore susceptible to operant conditioning. Behaviour modification has also been extended with success to autistic (unable to respond to and form relationships with others) and mentally retarded children to improve social skills (Williams, *et al.*, 1975) and table manners (Plummer *et al.*, 1977).

Reinforcers might include praise, attention and some tangible rewards such as special food, sweets or toys. These are **primary reinforcers** which the child has instant access to and can enjoy immediately. For example, Lovaas *et al.* (1973) developed a programme to modify the behaviour of autistic children from withdrawal to talking and social interaction. Initially, appropriate responses were rewarded with sweets. Later, when the children became more responsive, cuddling was used as a reinforcement for 'good' behaviour. Non-reinforcers included ignoring the child's inappropriate behaviour. (Getting cross with a child, shouting or smacking involve giving the child attention and might therefore act as a reinforcement of undesirable behaviour).

Token Economy Programmes Token economy systems are a form of behaviour modification and are often used in residential care settings. They are based on the principles of **secondary reinforcement** (see page **86**) where the rewards are not immediately available but are given in the form of tokens which can be exchanged later for **primary** (or direct) reinforcements such as sweets, extra outings or watching a favourite TV programme. This technique is generally used with adults or older children, who can make the association between the immediate, non-usable reinforcer and the later, more direct reinforcer.

There seems no doubt that token economy systems can be used effectively to train individuals to develop more acceptable behaviour. Kazdin (1977) claimed that programmes can be easily adapted to deal with individual problems such as self-care, participation in group exercises and improved domestic skills. In a hospital setting, Paul and Lentz (1977) compared the use of token economy techniques with milieu therapy (where residents are kept busy 85 per cent of their waking hours) and routine hospital procedures. They found that over a period of approximately five years, both token economy and milieu therapy patients reduced symptomatic behaviour more than the routine group. More token economy patients were discharged to community placements and were better at remaining in their placements than were members of the other two groups. However, a number of doubts and problems have been identified:

1. The new behaviours may not be generalised to the 'real world' situation. Baddeley (1990) has argued that in an educational environment children might only participate in a particular educational exercise, such as reading, if they were rewarded for it within the realms of the token economy system.
2. Within a setting such as an institution for children with special learning difficulties there may be special problems. It is important that whilst each child receives an individualised programme according to his or her needs, the pattern of reinforcements should be equitable so that unwanted rivalry does not develop. Also, reinforcements must be kept the same by all people who have dealings with the individuals. Devising such programmes can be time-consuming and difficult to achieve.
3. It has been suggested that token economy systems are effective for reasons other than reinforcement of the behaviour of participants in a programme. Other factors such as improved staff morale may be at least partly responsible. Fonagy and Higgitt (1984) pointed out that reinforcement of *staff* in care settings has been linked to improved client behaviour. Thus there is no absolute proof that the effectiveness of token economies is linked exclusively to principles of operant conditioning.

Behaviour Therapy

Behaviour therapy, based on the principles of classical conditioning, aims to change involuntary or reflex behaviour (see page **81**) which itself has been learned through the process of classical conditioning. Pavlov's dogs salivated when a buzzer sounded because initially the buzzer had been associated with the presentation of food; a child may learn to fear visits to the doctor because one visit became associated with the pain of an injection.

The term 'behaviour therapy' includes a number of techniques which are commonly used to treat such disorders as obsessive compulsive behaviour (an anxiety disorder where an individual feels compelled to repeat a stereotyped action or movement) or phobias (irrational fear). All the techniques assume that maladaptive behaviour has resulted from faulty learning, where the client has formed an association between two stimuli, one of which was perceived as threatening to them. Some of these techniques are discussed below.

Systematic Desensitisation   This technique is commonly used to treat relatively mild phobias. Clients are first taught to relax and then shown pictures of their feared object or problem. Gradually, the feared object is introduced in a step-by-step process until the client can tolerate actual contact with the object without anxiety. Many researchers have testified to the effectiveness of systematic desensitisation as a therapeutic technique (Rachman and Wilson, 1980; McGlyn *et al.*, 1981).

Aversion Therapy   This technique is used mainly to treat addictions or other unwanted behaviour. The aim is to attach negative feelings to stimuli which are considered inappropriately attractive. For example, if an emetic is paired with alcohol, the next alcoholic drink becomes less attractive. In some situations, electric shocks have been used as part of the 'pairing'. However, ethical questions have been raised and the practice has been discouraged.

Covert sensitisation is similar to aversion therapy but clients are asked to **imagine** their attractive stimuli and accompanying negative states such as electric shocks or vomiting. This to some extent deals with the ethical problem of unpleasant stimulus pairings.

Implosion Therapy and Flooding   Used mainly in the treatment of phobias the essence of both these therapies is to expose the client at the outset of treatment to their most feared situation. The premise is 'fighting fear with fear'. It seems to work in two ways:

1. Once clients have been exposed to the most horrific situation over a period of about an hour, their anxiety levels become exhausted. This is known as stimulus satiation.
2. Extinction of the client's fear responses occurs because the usual route of escape or avoidance is blocked by the therapist.

In **implosion therapy** the therapist elaborates the situation by constructing stories and outrageous scenarios. For example, the spider phobic may be asked to imagine a giant spider who devours their eyes and eats its way into the brain! Thus, implosion therapy affects the client's *imagination,* whereas **flooding** takes place *in vivo* (in a real life situation). For example, Wolpe (1958) took a patient with a fear of cars for a four-hour car journey. The girl became hysterical as her anxiety levels rose, but eventually became calm, and by the end of the journey her fears had disappeared.

A number of criticisms have been made regarding behaviour therapies:

1. Systematic desensitisation seems a relatively benign technique. It is difficult to realise that flooding, implosion and aversion therapy stem from the same theoretical position. There are serious questions about the ethics of using these strenuous methods, especially if they are no more effective than less traumatic methods. Supporters of flooding and implosion therapy claim that it is effective (Marks, 1981; Barratt, 1969). It is quick and therefore less costly for the client than other protracted therapies. However, the cost to the client may not only be in monetary terms and some therapists suggest that these should be used only when other means fail.

2. Aversion therapy is not often used nowadays for alcohol-related problems, as pairings have to be continually repeated in order to be effective and other methods have been found more successful. Also, there are ethical controversies about whether therapists should hurt people with electric shocks, even when those people have requested the treatment. It is possible they may be requesting punishment rather than treatment. For example, the treatment was at one time used for

homosexuals. Electric shocks were paired with photographs of attractive men. The effectiveness of this treatment has never been satisfactorily proven and the practice has now ceased for ethical reasons. Some investigations have failed to show any superiority of aversion therapy over a placebo (a form of treatment which, unknown to the client, is not expected to have any effect on their condition) (Diament and Wilson, 1975).

General Evaluation of Behavioural Therapies

Advantages
- As has already been noted, many studies have offered testimony to the general success of behavioural therapies. It could be argued that such techniques improve the quality of life for many individuals who suffer from such problems as phobias, obsessive compulsive disorders and poor personal and social skills. Marks (1981) concluded that behavioural therapies were the preferred choice for the treatment of about 25 per cent of non-psychotic complaints.

Criticisms
- The focus of behavioural therapies is on the 'here and now'. The client's actual behaviour is taken to be the essence of his or her problem. Such therapies have been criticised on the grounds that they only change overt behaviour and do not root out underlying causes. Therefore, the patient's problem may still exist and symptom substitution may occur (another maladaptive behaviour may be substituted).
- Behavioural therapies have been criticised on ethical grounds in that they aim to remove unacceptable behaviours and substitute acceptable behaviours. Decisions on what is and is not acceptable rest with the therapists. Do therapists have the right to make decisions which may have a profound effect on other people's lives?

> Behaviour modification appears to offer a technology by which we can help people, but we cannot dominate them. Long may that state of affairs continue. (Baddeley, 1990)

2. Biofeedback

This technique draws mainly on the principles of operant conditioning, Individuals are trained to control bodily processes such as heart rate and blood pressure, which are autonomic responses and not normally under voluntary control. Typically, patients are connected to a machine which gives a continuous reading of heart rate and blood pressure. They are trained to relax and are asked to consciously try to reduce one or both. When the readout falls to a given target level, a bell or tone sounds. The patient aims to maintain that level. The reinforcement for hypertensive patients in doing this, is the knowledge that they are helping to improve their own health.

Biofeedback techniques developed from studies using rats. Miller and DiCara (1967) showed that animals paralysed by the use of a curare could control their breathing rate and other autonomic functions if given a reward in the form of direct electrical brain stimulation. This was a particularly interesting finding because up to then it had been believed that autonomic functions could only be affected through the process of classical conditioning and that operant conditioning applied only to voluntary behaviour.

Initial results with human participants were encouraging, but biofeedback has not been established as a standard treatment for raised blood pressure (Shapiro and Surwit, 1979). Blanchard *et al.* (1979) believes that relaxation training is more effective. Added to this, it might be necessary for individuals to change their life-styles in order to effectively lower blood pressure in the 'real world' situation, rather than use biofeedback and assume that a 'cure' has been effective.

Various forms of epilepsy have been treated by biofeedback: in one study patients were trained to increase cortical activity in the sensori-motor cortex of the brain. However, improvement was not sustained when training sessions lapsed (Sterman, 1973).

Neuromuscular disorders such as cerebral palsy, paralysis following stroke or poliomyelitis have been treated by biofeedback (Basmajian, 1977). Patients are informed by biofeedback of the firing of single muscle cells, and then trained to reactivate these. Neural pathways which are disordered are normally under voluntary control and should therefore be ideal for retraining by biofeedback techniques. In damaged tissue, signs of muscle movement are faint and need amplification: this therefore acts both as a reinforcement and as a prompt for further effort.

Biofeedback has many applications in behavioural medicine, but its applications are more limited than were originally thought. As with behavioural therapies discussed above, biofeedback might be 'curing' the overt behaviour but not the underlying cause.

3. Programmed Learning

Programmed learning is a method of instruction based on the principles of operant conditioning. It has been used in formal educational settings such as schools, colleges and universities, in the armed forces (where it has been widely used) and in industrial training settings. Its main advantage is that it allows individual learners to work through organised learning material at their own pace and to receive feedback on their achievements at regular intervals.

Early programmes were presented on teaching machines; more recently computers have been used as a medium and many textbooks and self-study materials have employed the techniques of programmed instruction.

Theoretical Background

In the mid-1920s, Pressey produced the first recognisable teaching machine which involved the presentation of small items of information followed by multiple choice answers (a number of answers, only one of which is correct). These were presented through a small window in a drum and students were required to press a key corresponding to the correct answer before a new question became available.

In 1954, Skinner applied his findings from animal conditioning to the production of the first **linear** teaching programme (see below). Traditional classroom teaching, he argued, was inefficient because it failed to take account of the different abilities and previous knowledge of a group of students; lessons could not move according to the needs and pace of individual learners.

The theoretical base of programmed learning drew on the following principles of operant conditioning:

1. A motivated learner's actions which are followed by rewards (that is, are **reinforced**) are likely to be repeated and learned. The reward should follow as swiftly as possible after the response.
2. Actions which are not reinforced are likely to disappear (become **extinguished**).

3. Behavioural patterns may therefore be **shaped** by the use of controlled stimuli. In other words, learning can take place as a result of a series of small steps leading to a desired outcome.

Skinner's Linear Programmes

Skinner's remedy to the shortcomings of traditional teaching was the linear programme, the main characteristics of which are:

1. Subject matter is arranged in very small steps, known as **frames**, which are presented to the learner in a logical sequence.
2. The learner is required to make a 'constructed response' usually by writing a word or phrase in response to a question. (Each step is so small that there is almost no likelihood that the response will be incorrect.)
3. For each correct response, the learner is given reinforcement in the form of **immediate feedback** on the accuracy of the response. In the case of an incorrect response (which should occur only rarely), the learner moves back to the item for another attempt before moving on.

The linear programme therefore is made up of a series of frames, each containing a small amount of information to which a learner must respond. Frames also contain the answer to the problem set in the preceding frame. Figure 3.7 illustrates a small extract from a possible linear programme on operant conditioning.

Branching programmes offer greater flexibility than linear programmes in that they provide a variety of different routes through the material, depending on the student's ability and level of understanding.

Evaluation of Programmed Learning

Strengths

Though programmed learning did not result in the revolutionary changes in teaching and learning envisaged by Skinner, it has been extremely effective in specific situations. Curzon (1980) claims that programmed learning seems to have been particularly useful in the following situations:

FIGURE 3.7

An Extract from a Linear Programme on Operant Conditioning

Frame 1   Associative learning is one of the most basic forms of learning. It involves making a new connection or <u>as</u>_____ between events or stimuli in the environment

---

ASSOCIATION
Frame 2   Associative _____ means to make a new association between events or stimuli in the environment. Psychologists distinguish between two forms of associative learning: classical and operant conditioning

---

LEARNING
Frame 3   A dog buries a bone or chases a ball. Since these responses are voluntary and spontaneous, they are considered to be operant _____

RESPONSES
Frame 4   In operant conditioning we can increase the probability of a response being repeated if we reinforce it. Reinforcement can be anything which is likely to cause the behaviour to be _____

REPEATED
Frame 5   For example, if we want to teach a dog to 'shake hands' when we say 'Shake', we might lift its paw several times and on each occasion, give it a sweet. If the sweet causes the dog to repeat the 'shake hands' response, it can be called a _____

REINFORCEMENT

1. the learning of physical skills which lend themselves to being broken down into small steps: for example, some engineering processes;
2. the study of a subject for which there is a hierarchy of facts: for example, in mathematics or logic.

With the advent of computer-aided instruction, many effective programmes have been developed for use in a wide range of subjects in many different settings, from the primary school classroom to the business world.

In addition, the principles of programmed learning have been applied and are currently used in many textbooks and self-study materials. These have provided a useful method of study for individuals who are unable or who do not wish to attend conventional classes.

A study by Cavanagh (1963) compared programmed learning with conventional teaching in the training of technicians in the services. The main findings were:

- Achievement in both groups was similar.
- Students trained by programmed learning mastered the material more quickly than those taught by conventional methods.
- Retention and recall of learnt material was significantly better in the programmed learning group than in the conventionally taught group.

The findings from this study seems to suggest that programmed learning is a teaching and learning approach which has much to recommend it.

Criticisms

Critics have objected to Skinner's application to humans of principles drawn from animal conditioning. Human behaviour, it is argued, is too complex to be compared to the conditioning of rats and pigeons.

Perhaps the fundamental flaw in programmed learning which has prevented it from becoming the panacea expected by Skinner is its solitary nature which can lead to boredom and lack of motivation. Programmed learning does not provide opportunities for the stimulation and social support from fellow learners that can be found in the traditional classroom setting.

Self-Assessment Questions

1. Explain the main principles of operant conditioning on which programmes of behaviour modification are based.
2. Explain how token economy programmes differ from conventional programmes of behaviour modification. What doubts and problems have been identified in relation to token economy systems?
3. Discuss one form of behaviour therapy which is based on the principles of classical conditioning.
4. Critically evaluate the use of behavioural therapies.
5. Describe the main principles on which programmed learning is based. State some of the strengths and weaknesses in this approach to learning.

FURTHER READING

S. E. G. Lea, *Instinct, Environment and Behaviour* (London: Methuen, 1984).
A. Manning, and M. S. Dawkins, *Animal Behaviour* (Cambridge: Cambridge University Press, 1992)
S. Walker, *Learning Theory and Behaviour Modification* (London: Methuen, 1984).

Animal Communication 4

At the end of this chapter you should be able to:

1. Identify several ways in which animals respond to stimuli.
2. Appreciate the importance for animals' adaptation of *innate releasing mechanisms*.
3. Make an assessment of the effectiveness of intentional social communication.
4. Evaluate the significance of von Frisch's description of the honeybee dance.
5. Identify some of the criteria for language described by Hockett and others.
6. Evaluate attempts to teach language to apes and other animals, including dolphins and a parrot.

SECTION I   THE BASES OF COMMUNICATION

Animals respond in a wide variety of ways to their environment. Features within this environment may have one or more of several effects, including:

1. Orientation
2. Eliciting a response from other animals
3. Arousal

Orientation   refers to the means whereby an animal responds to the basic physical characteristics of its environment. It perceives light, gravity, air, water currents and similar things and responds so as to be in the right relationship to them. A fish rests with its head into the current. Even in total darkness, rats have a righting reflex which keeps them upright in respect to gravity. Honey-bees guide themselves using the sun as a compass.

Eliciting a response   refers to the way in which responsive behaviour occurs in relation to what an animal perceives. Specific behaviour by another animal or a specific feature in the environment is related to particular behaviour on the part of an animal.

Arousal   refers to less specific responses. Each incoming sensory pathway has collaterals which connect to the **reticular formation**. This is a collection of nerve fibres at the base of the brain which connect via non-specific pathways to all the higher centres of the brain with the purpose of arousing them to action. An example is the 'priming' of responses found in the courting of doves. When a female dove sees a male courting, she undergoes hormonal changes which make her more ready to engage in nest building. However, this effect is not immediate. Her perceptions need to be repeated and to build up over several days before she comes to reproductive condition. Responses, first hormonal and then behavioural, are being made, not only specifically, in that the courtship results in nest building eventually, but also in terms of her arousal in a much more general sense. She becomes more receptive to what she perceives. Adler (1974) has provided examples of this phenomenon. He refers to 'pumps', which act over a long period to increase receptivity, and 'triggers', which produce an immediate and specific response. Suckling provides the 'trigger' to make the female rat produce milk for her offspring while the pregnant female's activity in licking and grooming her nipples has encouraged mammary gland growth. This is a 'pump' effect.

The Sensory World of Animals

It would be wrong to think of the world of animals as being the same as ours from the point of view of the sensory information they receive. In some instances the sensory world of animals extends beyond ours; in others not so far. Insects, for instance , have compound eyes which provide them with very different sensations from our own. Image formation is very rudimentary, but at the same time they have a very wide field of view and highly developed ability to detect movement. They can see colour but they have greater sensitivity into the ultra-violet end of the spectrum, with less sensitivity at the red end. Red is confused with black or dark grey. Bees are sensitive also to the plane of polarisation of light and can use this sensitivity to locate the sun's position even when it is obscured by cloud. Our own flicker fusion frequency is about 50 cycles per second. This means that any light which flickers faster than this is seen as a steady light. Insect eyes may have a flicker fusion frequency of up to 250 cycles per second. This means that a fluorescent tube, working on Alternating Current (AC) mains supply at 50 cycles per second, is seen by us as a steady light while insects will be able to perceive the flickering of the tube.

So much for the sensory world of insects, but mammals also have a different sensory world. A cat or a dog gains more of its information through smell. Griffin (1958) has shown that bats use an extraordinarily sensitive system of echo-location to locate objects and to hunt insects while they are flying.

Sign Stimuli

The use of **sign stimuli** enable animals to pick out of the available array of sensory information available to them at any one time those features to which they must respond. This is discussed fully in Chapter 2. Examples include:

- A male stickleback's responses to red colouring and to the swollen underbelly of the female.
- Hen turkeys' responses to the cheeping sound of their chicks. When they hear it they accept the chicks; deafened birds kill them.
- Minnows' panic reaction when any fish is scratched or wounded and there is blood in the water.

There are several things to be borne in mind about sign-stimuli:

1. The fact that something has been called a sign stimulus does not mean that the normal response to it *only* occurs in response to it.
2. There may be more than one sign stimulus which will elicit a particular response. For instance, as well as red colouring, a head-down threat posture by a male stickleback in another's

territory will evoke an aggressive response. This provocative position is added to the colouring to provoke an even stronger response than either of them separately. This additive effect is termed **heterogeneous summation**.

3. Where animals rely upon inherited behaviour, it is more important for the survival of the animal that it never misses making a response to the stimulus than that there should occasionally be false responses. Driving away rival males from its territory was found by Tinbergen (1951) to be so important to a male stickleback that it showed extreme responsiveness to red colouring, even to the extent of showing aggression towards red flowers falling on to the surface of the water, or towards a passing red bus.

4. Similarly animals must never fail to respond to sign stimuli provided by a predator or to the alarm calls of other individuals. The alarm calls of other species too may provide early warning of impending danger. The ideal alarm call needs to carry as far as possible as well as giving the predator the least chance of locating the author of the alarm call. This will mean a constant pitch and a graduated beginning and ending.

Social Signals

Animals are frequently responsive to sounds, scents and colours in other animals. Lorenz has suggested that these sounds, scents and colours have specially evolved in order to evoke these responses (Lorenz, 1958). The term he used for them was **releasers**. The point he made was that the releasers and the animals' responses to them have become mutually adapted to each other in the course of evolution, so much so that these **social signals** have almost become a form of language.

Baerends (1957, 1959) conducted a series of experiments which demonstrated the way in which herring gulls determine which eggs are there to be incubated and which might provide food to eat. So far as incubation is concerned, there is a strong preference for green colouring, but even more important than the colour of the egg is its speckling. The more speckled an egg is and the greater the contrast between the speckling and the background, the more the gull is impelled to roll the egg into the nest and incubate it. Other characteristics such as shape are unimportant. Square or cone-shaped 'eggs' are rolled into the nest, just so long as they are speckled. Green colouring and speckling are the releasers for incubating behaviour. In contrast to this, where gulls are engaged in robbing nests to eat the eggs a red or a blue background colour becomes the releaser. Eggs with a green background colouring are the least likely to be eaten, even though they may be just as conspicuous. In the same way speckling is not nearly as attractive to feeding gulls as it is to incubating ones.

Exaggerated Characteristics

Ethologists have adopted the technique of creating mock-ups of stimuli and then systematically changing characteristics of these stimuli to see which ones seem to be the most important in evoking responses. Frequently it has been discovered that where some characteristic has been exaggerated the response to it also becomes stronger. Tinbergen (1951) found, for instance, that an oyster catcher will attempt to brood a giant egg in preference to its own. The larger an egg is (within limits) the more it seems to stimulate incubation. Another example is that of the silver-washed fritillary butterfly (*Dryas paphia*), studied by Magnus (1958). As they fly by, females of this species display a flashing orange wing pattern which attracts the males. Magnus devised a revolving drum which flashed the requisite orange wing pattern and thereby attracted the male fritillaries. The normal wing-beat speed of the butterfly is about 8 beats per second. Magnus found that the faster the wing beat simulated on the drum the more attractive it was to the males, up to as high as 75 beats per second. But, of course, the characteristics which provide releasers are not just for this purpose and the evolution of supernormal stimuli might militate against these other purposes so as to provide for stronger responses. Increasing the wing-beat speed of fritillaries might make the females of this species more attractive to the males but at the expense of less-efficient flight. Perhaps the increased response to exaggerated stimuli simply reflects an increase in general arousal evoked by the larger stimulus rather than a specifically stronger releaser.

Selectivity in Responses

An animal must inevitably have evolved a system to enable it to respond to certain stimuli within its environment and to ignore the rest. The discussion of sign stimuli above implies a filtering system which operates to separate those stimuli to which it will be genetically programmed to respond from those which will be passed over. Besides it is quite beyond the capability of any animal's brain to process all the information presented through its senses. Barlow (1961) has calculated that there are roughly 3 million sensory nerve fibres entering the brain . Assuming that each of these nerve fibres represents a switch which can either be 'off' or 'on', the number of possible combinations of sensory input is astronomical. The brain has to economise in handling sensory information and this implies that there must be a filter system. This filtering can occur at one of two points:

1. There may be filtering **periphally** at the point where the information impinges upon the organism, through its senses. In humans this filtering in part takes the form of limitations in the sensitivity of the senses. We cannot hear sounds, for instance, above a frequency of about 20 kilohertz. It has already been noted that the sensitivity of human eyes falls short of being sensitive to ultra-violet light while honey-bees have greater sensitivity. That is to say, the peripheral filtering system of the honey-bee is different from ours.
2. There may also be **central filtering**. Selection of what stimuli are to be responded to, may be in the central rather than the peripheral nervous system, the brain rather than the senses. Lorenz (1937) has suggested that there might be a specific mechanism responsible for filtering out those stimuli to which the animal is genetically programmed to respond. He termed this the **innate releasing mechanism** (IRM).

Innate Releasing Mechanism (IRM)

How an IRM operates can be illustrated by an example. Tinbergen and Perdeck (1950) studied the pecking responses of gull chicks. An adult gull's bill is yellow with a red patch on the lower mandible. The aim of Tinbergen and his colleague was to establish what characteristic of this bill provided the stimulus for the chicks to peck at it and for the adult to regurgitate the food brought back to the nest. A number of cardboard models were made which varied the following attributes:

- head colour
- head shape
- bill colour
- the colour of the patch on the lower mandible
- the degree of contrast of the patch on a medium grey bill

Care was taken to present these models to the chicks in a standard manner. First, each type of model was presented to an equal number of chicks which had not seen a model or a real adult gull before. Then the order of presentation was randomised.

Results showed the patch on the mandible to be the crucial attribute. Contrast was important. Grey bills with black or white patches were responded to more than plain bills. Red colouring was important. A plain red bill attracted more responses than any other colour, and a red patch was responded to more than a black one even where there was less contrast. Head colour and head shape made no difference to the response. The central filter system seems to filter out redness and contrast and ignores bill colour, head shape and head colour. It is, however, still possible that filtering is peripheral. There is some evidence that blue light appears darker to birds' eyes than an equivalent quantity of red light and so might be more likely to seize the chick's attention.

Alarm Responses

A factor which may contribute to the survival of a species is its ability to recognise and respond to the presence of possible predators. Certain species of birds – ducks, geese, pheasants and turkeys, for instance – raise alarm calls when a bird of prey passes overhead. Individuals with young can then respond by providing shelter. Turkey hens spread their tails as they give the alarm signal and the young chicks come and find shelter beneath them.

In other species alarm signals may take different forms. Among insects, alarm systems are often chemical. Maschwitz (1964, 1966) surveyed 23 species of *Hymenoptera* and found evidence of alarm pheromones in all of them. Carl (1971) in his study of arctic ground squirrels (*Spermophilus undulatus*) found that it was impossible to come close to groups of animals who set up waves of alarm calls which increased in intensity and duration as an intruder approached. On the other hand he was able to approach to within three metres of an individual squirrel. They clearly found safety in numbers. There is some evidence that an alarm pheromone exists among rodents. Carr *et al.* (1970), among others, found that house mice produce an odour when they are under stress which causes avoidance by some other animals. Responses to alarm signals differ markedly between species, some displaying aggression and some panic flight. Wilson and Regnier (1971) found both of these reactions among formicine ants. Some species orient themselves aggressively towards the source of the problem while others scatter in all directions in panic.

The chances are that the recipients of these alarm calls will be related to the caller. The apparent altruism of an animal drawing attention to itself to give warning of an intruder serves to enhance the chances of some of the animal's genes surviving. If the warning enables more than two of its brothers or sisters to survive, or more than eight of its cousins (a brother carries 50 per cent of its genes, a cousin 12.5 per cent), then the sacrifice of the calling animal's life will have been worthwhile in evolutionary terms. This has been fully discussed in Chapter 1.

Self-Assessment Questions

1. Describe three ways in which an animal may respond to the physical nature of its environment. Discuss some of the functions of these responses.
2. In what ways is the sensory world of animals different from our own?
3. Describe some of the main functions of sign stimuli.
4. In what ways have animals become mutually adapted to one another? How do the social signals they employ contribute to this adaptation?
5. What seem to be the main functions of innate releasing mechanisms?

SECTION II   SOCIAL COMMUNICATION

So far in this chapter we have been concerned with the way in which animals respond to what they perceive in the environment in which they live. To say that an animal is communicating requires also that there is an element of purposiveness. An animal must *intend* to pass information to another, rather than simply receiving and responding to a signal within its environment. This does not necessarily mean that the intention needs to be conscious; it involves a mutual adaptation between the communicating animals to the benefit of both. Again communication will often be between members of the same species, but it does not need to be confined to this. When a skunk raises its tail and presents its hindquarters to a potential predator it passes information to it; as the saying goes – 'Nemo me impune lacessit', which roughly translated means 'No one gets away scot-free with harassing me!'

Even within this overall definition of what is meant by social communication there can be variants. Altmann (1962) has a broad definition: 'a process by which the behaviour of an individual affects the behaviour of others'. This clearly applies to the skunk. Hinde and Rowell (1962) limit their definition somewhat to those visual signals which clearly had evolved for the purpose of affecting the behaviour of others.

Modes of Communication

Different groups of animals seem to have specialised modes of communication which relate to the evolution of their sense modalities. These can include tactile communication, sound, chemical and visual signals.

Tactile Communication

Tactile communication is important among many invertebrates, for instance among earthworms emerging from their burrows at night to mate, or among social insects. Among higher species, when one monkey spends time grooming another it is conveying general information about the social relationship which exists between the animals. There are clearly limitations on tactile communication. It can by its nature only be used at close range. Feeler range is about as far as it can go.

Sound Signals

Where it is advantageous to communicate over longer distances and perhaps through obstacles, such as dense vegetation, sound is a more appropriate mode. Hooker and Hooker (1969) have described the way in which the African bou-bou shrike use low flute-like calls. While remaining concealed in dense vegetation the male and the female of this species conduct a kind of duet of alternating calls to one other. Low notes seem to have the characteristic of carrying through the undergrowth over great distances. The study by Payne and McVay (1971) into the 'song' of humpback whales has suggested that their communication can be received hundreds of miles away. Water is a better medium for sound communication than is air.

Chemical Signals

Both insects and mammals use chemical communication, though there are limitations. Patterning is not possible, as it is with sound or visual signalling, and it is not easy to turn the signal off and on quickly. The information conveyed in this way needs to be relatively stable as well as relatively simple. 'This is my territory' is the message conveyed by mammals marking the limits of their territory; or 'I am ready to mate' when female animals secrete special chemicals to indicate their receptivity to the male. These chemical signals referred to as **pheromone** are supposed to stimulate reproductive urges. Indeed, one kind have recently been incorporated into 'scent' marketed by a cosmetics firm. It is believed that they are important in human communication also. Wilson (1965) has described the way in which chemical signals are adapted to their purpose. Pheromone and territorial signals need to persist well, so they consist of chemicals which are not too volatile. Where some insects use chemicals to signal alarm, persistence needs to be less. Consequently they can be more volatile.

Visual Signals

The range of visual signals must inevitably be fairly short. Alarm signals often involve flashes of white which can be seen over quite long distances. The white underside of the tails of rabbits are an instance. Colour is quite important among fish, reptiles and birds, though less important among mammals, with the exception of primates including humans.

Message or Meaning

There are a number of separate issues related to message and mean-ing, including:

- **Purpose and intention.** A male bird singing in its own territory may be conveying information about his present condition.
- **Interpretation.** How the receiver interprets the message may be more than this. It may include information not only about the sender's state but where he is, whether he has a mate and even who he is.
- **Consciousness.** Some of this information may be consciously conveyed, other information unconsciously conveyed. In a simi-lar fashion, humans convey certain information by what they say, and more information by non-verbal signals (what they are wearing, what postures they adopt, what gestures and what tone of voice they use).

Information conveyed includes:

- **Sexual information**: Pheromones, for example, convey infor-mation about the transmitter's state.
- **Information between parents and offspring**: Food calls or alarm signals are examples.
- **Contact signals**: These are important for animals who live in groups: such calls are made by geese in flight. Lorenz (1952) describes the way in which a flock of geese on the ground take the decision to fly. One bird (or a few) begins to call. If this call to flight is taken up generally, then the flock will take to the wing. If too few respond the flock remains on the ground.

Meta-Communication

Where the intention of a message is to qualify other signals which follow it, this has been termed **meta-communication**. Some carni-vores (lions or dogs, for instance) invite their young to play with them. Forequarters are lowered as an indication that all apparently aggressive movements which follow are in fact only in play. Dogs sometimes also wag their tails during play fights. This kind of playful rehearsal of aggression is evolutionarily necessary. Young animals can be trained to stalk and attack without the risk of engaging in real fighting.

Pumps or Triggers

Some signals are 'all or nothing', while others allow for a graded response. Brown (1964) found that Steller's jays (*Cyanocitta stelleri*) provide information regarding the amount of resistance which may be expected in case of an invasion of territory by the way in which their crests are held. If the bird intends to flee or if the approach is part of courtship then the crest is held flat. Otherwise the higher the angle at which the crest is held, the greater the resistance which is to be expected. Leyhausen (1956) attempted to grade the facial expressions of cats according to their aggressiveness and to their fear (see Figure 4.1).

The problem with this kind of signal is that it can be ambiguous to the receiver. In many cases it makes better sense to have a stereotyped signal. Alarm calls need to be of a fixed kind, as do sexual signals in many cases. Many signals have a pump effect in that they may be repeated on many occasions and over successive days, so that their effects gradually increase and make the receiver more likely to respond. Animals lacking as they do the resources of a symbolic language system have to rely upon context and upon the way in which signals are combined to convey their meaning. Attempts have been made, which will be described in detail later, to teach symbolic language to primates. However, in the wild, in spite of the fact that their social interactions may be quite complex, they exhibit very few gestures. While human beings frequently attempt to deceive those with whom they are communicating this seems nearly impossible for animals. Where there seems to be deceit, as in the case of the moth with eye spots, these spots are simply visual releasers, evolved to deceive predators.

Effectiveness of Social Communication in Animals

The only way to be certain that animal communication works is to be able to measure responses to it. We have already seen some examples of the measurement of communication in animals. Tinbergen's experiments with the red spot on a herring gull's bill, mentioned above, are illustrative of attempts to measure *visual*

FIGURE 4.1

Expression of Fear and Aggressiveness in Cats (after Leyhausen, 1956)

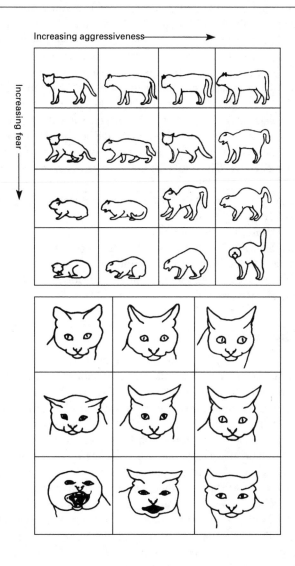

communication. Clearly, the response of the chicks to various stimuli presented to them shows whether or not the communication has been received. Noble (1936) studying yellow-shafted flickers (*Colaptes auratus*), a type of American woodpecker in which the only obvious difference between males and females is a small black mark or moustache beside the bill, captured the female of a pair of flickers and stuck a moustache of black feathers on to her. When she was returned to her mate she had a very rude reception. She was promptly attacked and driven from the male's territory, not to be accepted again until the moustache had been removed. The moustache was clearly a communication to the male of this species of woodpecker that here was a rival who had to be driven from the territory.

It is difficult to measure how effective a signal has been. For instance, if there is no response it may not simply mean that that signal is ineffective. There may be one of several reasons; for instance:

- The receiver may have received the message but failed to respond for some reason.
- The signal was not perceived.
- The signal may act not so much as a trigger to set off a preconditioned response (as with the herring gull chicks), but as a 'pump' which has the effect of altering the perceiver's receptivity to subsequent signals.

The Honey-Bee Dance

Research by von Frisch (1967) has stimulated a great deal of discussion on the subject of animal communication, particularly relating to problems of measurement. It was known for a long time that bees must have some form of communication relating to flower crops, but it was von Frisch's careful observations which elaborated upon the dance system which bees seem to use to convey information about the nature and whereabouts of food sources.

Von Frisch marked foraging bees as they drank from prepared dishes of sugar syrup and then observed their behaviour as they returned to the hive. For the purposes of this observation glass-sided observation hives were used. On its return to a hive, a forager contacts other bees on the surface of the comb and gives up its cropful of sugar syrup to them. Then the dance begins. If the food source is within 50 metres of the hive, the bee performs what has become known as the *round dance*. Staying in approximately the same place on the comb, the bee moves alternately to the right and to the left over a circular path. Other bees face the dancer, sometimes in contact with her through their antennae. This round dance seems to be the signal which conveys the information 'leave the hive and search within 50 metres'.

When the food source (in von Frisch's experiments, his dishes of sugar syrup) was moved beyond 50 metres, the forager's dance changed its form. Between the turns to left and to right a series of short runs was incorporated with the bee waggling its abdomen rapidly from side to side. It is from this waggle dance – von Frisch claims – that much more information is transmitted and read back by other bees who follow every move the dancer makes. Work by Esch *et al.* (1965) suggests that bees also produce bursts of high-pitched sound during the waggling dance. The waggling dance remains essentially the same whether the food source is 100 metres distant or 5 kilometres. Distance is indicated by the tempo of the dance. There are 9–10 complete cycles of dance per 15 seconds when the food is 100 metres away, and this speed of dance falls off steeply at first and then more gradually until at 6 kilometres there are only 2 cycles of dance per 15 seconds. In addition to this there are correlations between the distance the food source is away and the number of waggles and the duration of each waggle. As the distance increases both the number of waggles and the duration of each waggle increase.

However, it is perhaps the way in which the *direction* of the food source is indicated which is the most remarkable. Von Frisch discovered by means of repeated observations at different times of the day that bees as they forage record the direction of the food source relative to the sun. As they perform their dances on a vertical comb when the sun is not visible, this angle to the sun is transposed to the same angle relative to gravity. The waggle run is, for instance, 10 degrees to the left of the vertical where the angle of the food source relative to the sun is 10 degrees to the left of it. It follows that as the sun apparently moves across the sky, so the angle of the bees' dance, relative to gravity, will change.

Some Qualification of von Frisch's Findings

While von Frisch and his co-workers were convinced that the bee dance represented a form of communication between foraging bees and those which remained in the hive, Wells and Wenner (1973) have disagreed with this interpretaion. Their hypothesis was that the dance merely stimulated bees to go out and forage. The food source was then located by smell. While they do not disagree with von Frisch's observations with regard to the form of the dance and the apparent relationship to the distance and direction of the food source, they assert that this information is not communicated to the other bees in the hive. They paid more attention to the scents which adhered to the bodies of foragers from the food source and to the wind direction. Bees in the hive were given a choice of food source.

• Some dishes were scented and placed at sites some distance from the hive. These had previously been visited and indicated by dances even though the scent had now been lost.
• Other dishes also at some distance away from the hive were scented, but had not previously been visited or indicated by the dance ritual.

It was predicted that if a large number of bees made the second of these choices, Wells and Wenner's olfactory theory was a more likely explanation than von Frisch's dance-language theory. This turned out to be the case. Additionally, it turned out that the direction of the wind was significant and this was not noted in von Frisch's experiments.

The important point about this in relation to animal communication is that it is very hard to show that communication has occurred unless the recipients of the message respond. Wenner's research seemed to show that the bees were not responding to the dances but to other cues. If Wenner's explanation is accepted then the relationship between the food source and the nature and form of the dance (which seems to be proven) does not have any obvious function.

Gould *et al.* (1985) have produced a very elegant solution to the problem. It was discovered some years ago that if there was a small point of light to the side of a vertical comb, the bees took this to be the sun. When dancing a bee will treat this point of light in exactly the same way as it would treat the sun. A food source at, say, 10 degrees to the left of the sun is indicated by a waggle-run at a similar angle in relation to the point of light. If this light is not available then the bees orient their dances in relation to gravity, as we have seen (p. 135). Gould blacked out the ocelli (simple eyes) on the dorsal surface of the bees' heads, so they then required a much stronger light source before they could respond. Gould made ocelli-blackened bees perform their dances on a comb with a very dim light source, so that they behaved as though there were no light and related their waggle-run to gravity. Watching bees with undamaged sight could therefore be misled (they took the light source, invisible to the dancers, as the sun) and would appear at dishes set out in a fan array according to the apparent angle indicated. The light on the comb was moved every 30 minutes. The angle apparently indicated therefore moved also. Gould also had all the ocelli-blackened dancers anaesthetised as they arrived at the dishes.

The results of this experiment showed clearly that Wells and Wenner's olfaction theory was mistaken and that von Frisch's dance-language hypothesis was correct. As the light source was moved so the new recruits among the bees shifted their attention to dishes displaced by an equivalent angle. It appears fairly certain that communication does occur by means of the dance. The important point is that measurement of whether communication occurs must depend upon the observed behaviour of those receiving the communication. There is further discussion of animal communication in Chapter 3 in relation to learning and in the final section of this chapter which discusses attempts that have been made to teach animals human language.

More recently still, Michelsen and his colleagues have gone further towards demonstrating that von Frisch was right (Michelsen, 1989; Michelsen *et al.*, 1989). They constructed a brass model which they placed in the hive and allowed to become covered with beeswax. In this way it acquired the odour of the colony. The model could be moved through the waggle dance in simulation of the bee dance and even had an artificial 'wing' which simulated the acoustic field around the real bee dancer when it was vibrated. It was successful in that foragers were induced to visit dishes of food not previously visited and the directions they move in and the distances they travel correspond to the 'dance' pattern of the model.

Self-Assessment Questions

1. In what ways may animals purposively convey information as a form of social communication?

2. What sorts of information are conveyed in this way?
3. What evidence have we for the effectiveness of this kind of social communication?
4. Make some assessment of the significance of von Frisch's investigation of the honey-bee dance.

SECTION III TEACHING HUMAN LANGUAGE TO ANIMALS

Introduction: What Is Language?

Before discussing attempts which have been made to teach human language to animals, it is as well to be clear about what constitutes language. Is it just communication as described in the earlier parts of this chapter? Or is it a wholly different order of things? Brown (1973) has claimed that language has been a critical attribute of human beings for between one and three million years. This is quite impossible to establish beyond doubt. There are no fossil remains (or indeed other remains) which provide evidence of *spoken* language going back to an early date. Writing systems (which can of course leave remains) go back some six thousand years.

Clark and Malt (1984) have suggested that a fully-fledged language has to have the following attributes:

1. It has to be reasonably regular in form so that it can readily be learned by children.
2. Because spoken words disappear so quickly from our echoic memory (the most immediate and most basic form of retention) it must be possible to interpret what is spoken very rapidly.
3. It must be capable of capturing those ideas which people want to convey. It follows that there is a very close relationship between the context in which people live and the language which they speak. To take an example of this, human beings are sensitive (because of the nature of their visual system) to four primary colours – red, green, blue and yellow. Where language has a limited number of terms to depict colours, these four colours are always included.
4. Language must be able to function in a social setting. It must be an aid to the social relationships between people.

Hockett (1959, 1960) proposed a number of criteria for defining human language. First there were several 'design features', as he termed them, which seem appropriate enough for human spoken language, but are less applicable to written language or to other non-spoken forms of human language (for example, sign language as used by the deaf, semaphore or morse signalling systems or perhaps even the 'tick-tack' code used by bookies on race courses).

- **Vocal/auditory character**: Language is seen as carried by sound, made vocally and received auditorily.
- **Broadcast transmission and directional reception**: Language is broadcast and the receiver must be able to tell where it comes from.
- **Rapid fading**: Vocal language fades rapidly.
- **Feedback**: It must be possible for someone using language to hear what he/she is saying.

Hockett also included a number of design features which have become accepted as criteria by which language production by animals may be judged. These include the following:

- **Interchangeabilty**: Language is a two-way process of communication with speakers able both to send and receive information.
- **Specialisation**: The speech function is for communication only and is not a by-product of any other form of behaviour.
- **Semanticity**: Language conveys meaning.
- **Traditional transmission**: This refers to the possibility of transferring language skills from one generation to the next.
- **Learnability**: Language can be learned.
- **Discreteness**: Information is coded not by the length of the utterance but by the position of the phonemes (the units of utterance).
- **Displacement**: This involves the ability to convey information about things which are not present in time or place.
- **Duality of patterning**: There is a double pattern to language. Words are made up of phonemes, sentences of words.
- **Productivity**: A user of language is capable of generating an infinite number of novel utterances.
- **Prevarication**: Language can be used to talk about impossible things or things that are not true.

● **Reflexiveness**: Language can be used to talk about language.

Brown (1973) has selected three of these features as essential for language: **semanticity, productivity** and **displacement**. We shall discuss further the extent to which those who have attempted to teach human language to apes and other species have been successful in meeting these criteria.

How far do these criteria go towards suggesting that animal communication is in fact the use of *language*? Much of what has been discussed so far in this chapter is not so much language as signalling. It falls down especially on the criterion of displacement. Von Frisch's account of the honey-bee dance, however, does seem to be an exception. Information is passed to other worker bees about the location of nectar which may be at some distance from the hive. But even if it passes the criterion of displacement other of Hockett's criteria do not seem to apply. For example, there is no evidence for prevarication. Bees convey information about where the sources of food are, not where there are no sources of food. Productivity also is lacking. The dances are set patterns and there is no way in which an infinite number of novel utterances may be generated .

Teaching Human Language to Other Species

Attempts have been made over many years to show that the use of language was not a species-specific attribute of humans but was a result of human intelligence. It was argued that if this was the case it ought to be possible to teach animals who were close to humans on the phylogenetic scale (chimpanzees and gorillas particularly) to use language. An early attempt by the Kelloggs (Kellogg and Kellogg, 1933) was a complete failure. The chimpanzee 'Gua' was not able to utter a single word despite being brought up with the Kelloggs' own child and treated exactly alike. She was, however, capable of understanding about 70 words or commands.

Keith and Cathy Hayes (Hayes 1951, Hayes and Hayes 1952) used operant conditioning to teach their chimpanzee, Vicki, to talk. This too seems to have been a failure. The problem was that chimpanzees lack the vocal apparatus to make the sounds of human speech. Taking account of this a number of researchers began a different approach. Gardner and Gardner (1969) used American Sign Language (ASL) as a medium. They appear to have had much greater success with 'Washoe', a female chimpanzee. ASL uses gestures to represent words and there are also devices to indicate verb tense and other grammatical structures. The Gardners created an environment for Washoe that was as close as possible to that which might obtain in a household where the parents were deaf. They signed to Washoe and to each other in her presence and rewarded correct gestures by the chimp. By the time Washoe was four she had mastered 160 signs. The following positive results were obtained:

- She was able to generalise. A sign representing a particular object or activity might be used for a similar one. She even overgeneralised as young children often do.
- She also began at a fairly early stage to string signs together; at first, just two signs together. Braine (1963) has described the way in which young children string words together in terms of **pivot** and **open** words. For example, in utterances like 'milk allgone' and 'Sarah sleep', 'allgone' and 'sleep' are pivot words which can be combined with a number of different open words. Washoe combined signs in a similar fashion.
- There was even some evidence of displacement in Washoe's signing. There were times when she seemed to be referring to objects which were not physically present.
- She was even able to recombine signs to express new meanings. She was shown a swan and asked 'What's that?' She replied 'Water bird'.

At first sight it seems that Washoe developed a 'language' which met at least some of Hockett's criteria, but there does need to be some caution:

1. There is a danger of anthropomorphising (treating Washoe's behaviour as though it was that of a human). While she used some of the signs used by a deaf person there is no way of knowing whether they had the same meaning to her as they would have had to a human. Semanticity is difficult to prove.
2. Many of the gestures which she learnt were those which were natural to apes in any case. There is a great deal of overlap in the gestural repertoire of Washoe and of untrained apes.
3. Washoe only mastered the hand configurations of American Sign Language. Signs used in ASL are defined in terms of four

parameters – hand configuration, movement, orientation and location. The Gardners seem to have focused only on the first of these.

4. In relation to syntax, Washoe seems to have developed a consistency in the way in which she combined signs which might indicate an understanding of syntax. However, Terrace *et al.* (1979) carried out a detailed analysis of the 35 multi-sign sequences which Washoe used in the film *Teaching Sign Language to the Chimpanzee, Washoe*. All of them were preceded by a prompt from the teacher, so the ordering of signs might have been purely imitative and not due to a mastery of syntax.

The success of the Gardners with Washoe prompted others to make similar efforts to train primates to use forms of language. Patterson (1978) trained Koko, a gorilla, and made the claim that 'language is no longer the exclusive domain of man'.

An alternative approach was adopted by Premack and Premack (1972,) who developed an artificial language of symbols (plastic shapes which could be attached to a magnetic board) and taught it to an ape, Sarah. She made significant progress. She certainly seemed to have some understanding of the relationship between the symbols and the meanings they represented. She also seemed to understand the significance of word order in expressions like 'red on green' or 'green on red'. She could arrange coloured cards to correspond with a sentence or construct a sentence to describe the way the cards were arranged. She could construct sentences containing the verb '*be*', and use the conjunction '*and*' as well as terms for colour, shape and size. She was able to follow commands from a sentence of symbols that represented such things as 'Sarah, put the banana in the pail and the apple in the dish.' When she was shown two objects, a key and a pencil for instance, and the symbols for them, she could correctly pick the correct symbol for 'same' or 'not same' 80 per cent of the time.

A chimp, Lana, was taught to communicate on a computer keyboard by punching symbolic keys. More recently, Savage-Rumbaugh *et al.* (1983) studied a pygmy chimp called Kanzi who learned symbols by watching other chimps being trained. Kanzi learned to combine symbols, make statements and ask for things. When another chimp, Austin, was removed from Kanzi's compound he typed the symbols for Austin and TV and was then quite happy to watch a videotape of Austin (*New York Times*, 1985). There is some evidence that all these animals have acquired complex skills. It is much more difficult to assess whether this amounts to language acquisition. Terrace (1979) attempted to teach language to a chimpanzee called Nim Chimpsky (a pun upon the name of Noam Chomsky, the linguist who has been foremost among those who claim language to be a species-specific capacity in humans). Between the ages of 18 months and three years Nim was observed to have used more than 19,000 'utterances' consisting of two or more signs. Analysing these two sign combinations, Terrace and his co-workers found that of combinations consisting of a verb and either 'me' or 'Nim' the chimpanzee chose in 83 per cent of cases to put the verb first – 'hug Nim' rather than 'Nim hug'.

Comparisons with Human Children's Speech

An analysis of children's speech when they start to produce two-word combinations has shown that in about 80 per cent of cases their utterances are in one of eight semantic categories – action + object, for instance 'drink milk', or object + beneficiary, 'food Sarah'. Terrace found that 84 per cent of Nim's 'utterances' fell into one of these semantic categories.

So far it looks as though Nim's utterances show a striking similarity to those of young children. However, while children rapidly develop throughout the period between two and four years old from producing two-word utterances to stringing sentences together of four words or more, Nim remained stuck with two-word utterances. While children's three or four-word utterances extend the meaning of what they are trying to say beyond what they could say in two words, Nim's three-word combinations often did little more than repeat or emphasise. So you find not 'Give Nim banana' but something more like 'banana Nim banana Nim'. Videotaped interactions of Nim's utterances revealed further differences between the chimp and the average child at a similar stage of language development.

1. Far more frequently than with human children, Nim's utterances interrupted signs which his handlers had been making. Instead of the **turn taking** which Trevarthen, among others, had noted in small children from babyhood (Trevarthen, 1974), Nim did not appear interested in making conversation.
2. When small children start to talk, about 20 per cent of their utterances are imitative of their parents' expressions, and about

30 per cent are spontaneous and not in response to something an adult has said. With Nim the proportions were 40 per cent imitative and only about 10 per cent could have been regarded as spontaneous. Nim used language in a markedly less creative and more imitative way than human children do.

Evaluation of Attempts to Teach Apes Human Language

The question at issue is this. Can it be said with any degree of assurance that language is not a species-specific capacity in humans? Or is it a function of intelligence which is related in turn to the position animals occupy on the phylogenetic scale? The answer rests in part upon the extent to which workers have been able to impart language (as defined by Hockett's criteria) to animals close to us on the phylogenetic scale. Of these criteria some are clearly not relevant to the use of ASL as a 'language' and can be discounted. The main design features with which we are concerned are therefore the following:

- Interchangeability
- Displacement
- Productivity
- Traditional transmission
- Prevarication
- Reflexiveness

1. **Interchangeability**: There is some evidence that chimps in a colony set up by Roger Fouts in Oklahoma (Fouts, 1972) showed interchangeability. Washoe went there after she left the Gardners. The animals freely gave and received signs among themselves even when there were no humans present.
2. **Displacement**: Washoe would sign 'time eat', which suggested she had a concept of time, and Fouts designed an experiment to demonstrate displacement. One chimp is taken out of the sight of the others and shown two hidden 'presents', one pleasant and one unpleasant (food, perhaps, and something chimps dislike – (a stuffed snake, for instance). Then the chimp is taken back to the other chimps and left for a while. Evidence of displacement was found in that the chimps managed to convey where the 'presents' were.
3. **Productivity**: Evidence from Terrace (1979) does not seem to

back claims for apes' productivity, but Koko, Patterson's gorilla (Patterson, 1979), seems to have devised her own form of swearing, 'You big dirty toilet!'

4. **Traditional transmission**: There does seem to be evidence that Washoe succeeded in passing her signing skills on to her children. Certainly, chimps seem to be able to learn signs from each other when they are living together.
5. **Prevarication**: Patterson describes what she claims is evidence for this. When she puts a stethoscope to her ears Koko smirks and puts her hands over her eyes.
6. **Reflexiveness**: Patterson described how Michael, a gorilla who lived with Koko, correctly copied signs made by Koko and was rewarded by Koko signing 'Good sign, Michael'.

All this seems rather inconclusive. The conclusion which Terrace has drawn is 'I can find no evidence confirming an ape's grammatical competence, either in my own data or those of others that could not be explained by other processes' (Terrace, 1979, p. 67).

The researchers themselves seem to be convinced that there is evidence for interchangeability, productivity, reflexiveness and prevarication. In an attempt to avoid bias in their results the Gardners used double blind techniques. Washoe had to make an appropriate sign for a series of photographic slides shown to her in random order. Another researcher who could see the slides was asked to record the signs which Washoe made. It is clear that if the signs made were clear enough for the observer to understand and this seemed to be the case, then Washoe must have understood the meaning of the signs and could name objects correctly. There is evidence of displacement in the account given by Patterson of a conversation with her gorilla, Koko, which took place three days after Koko had bitten Patterson:

Me: What did you do to Penny?
Koko: Bite.
Me: You admit it.
Koko: Sorry, bite, scratch. Wrong bite.
Me: Why bite?
Koko: Because mad.
Me: Why mad?
Koko: Don't know.

(Patterson, 1979, p. 459)

There remains the problem that apes do not seem to sign without prompting. Many apparently original signs made are in fact responses to questions or they are straightforward imitations of signs made to them. Their signs could be chains of operant responses which the apes use to get what they want from their trainers.

Experiments with Other Species

These include marine mammals such as dolphins and an African grey parrot. Batteau and Markey (1968) attempted to introduce an artificial language to dolphins and succeeded in testing the ability of dolphins to respond to simple commands given by artificially generated whistle words. However, owing to the death of Batteau this project was not completed and such detail as exists appears only in an unpublished government report.

Comprehension or Production of Language

Researchers in this area appear to have had a comprehension approach in mind, as opposed to the production approach adopted by the experimenters with apes, mentioned above. Herman and his coworkers (Herman *et al.*, 1984) have claimed that there is merit in concentrating upon comprehension rather than production as a critical measure of sentence processing. It is hard to assess the production of language by apes quantitatively or to be objective in the interpretation of what is produced. This is true even of the production of language by human children. The assumption that production implies comprehension is not necessarily valid. For example, the production of speech without meaning is a feature of some psychotic behaviour and has been termed **echolalia.** It involves the meaningless repetition of the last word that was heard. Production may easily be prompted by non-linguistic cues, as Terrace (1979) noted in his criticisms of the Gardners' work. He regarded grammatical structure as part of the essential definition of language and suggested that the Gardners had not conclusively shown Washoe's understanding of this. Much of what he observed in his detailed analysis of the Gardners' film of their work with Washoe could be explained by operant conditioning. A key human linguistic skill is the tacit use of grammatical features of a language to produce and comprehend sentences, including ones that are novel to the user.

Chomsky describes this 'mysterious ability' in the following terms:

> Having mastered a language, one is able to understand an indefinite number of expressions which are new to one's experience and one is able with greater or less facility to produce such expressions on an appropriate occasion. (Chomsky, 1972, p. 100)

In parallel with research where attempts were made to teach sign language to primates (Gardner and Gardner, 1969; Patterson, 1979; Terrace, 1979; etc.), Herman *et al.* (1984) taught dolphins to respond by using a 'language' which did not necessitate them having to produce the sounds of human speech. There were two versions of this 'language'. Their original experiments began in January 1977 with a dolphin (*Tursiops truncatus*) Keakiko ('Kea'). Sounds were generated by computer to represent each of three objects (a ball, a life ring and a styrofoam cylinder) and each of three actions (to fetch, to touch and to mouth). Kea was able to learn these. She was also was able to respond immediately to new objects which were instances of the class of old objects (new balls of different colours and textures, for example). She was also able immediately to generalise her action responses to new (and unnamed) objects introduced into the tank.

The way it worked was something like this. Two-word sentences were produced consisting of **object + action** (e.g. 'ball fetch'). The naming of the object first provided a bridge on which the action signal that followed was contingent. Kea was quite quickly able to respond flawlessly to each of the nine possible two-word sentences. Unfortunately, the project came to an abrupt end with the abduction of Kea. She and Puka, another dolphin in the same tank, were abducted and taken in a small van to a remote location where they were abandoned in the open sea. It is doubtful whether long-domesticated dolphins were able to survive the stress of removal from familiar surroundings to the wild.

A new project was begun in 1979 with two new female dolphins, Akeakamai and Phoenix. Akeakamai was taught to comprehend an acoustic language, while Phoenix was taught a gestural language. The 'languages' had a lexical component (words) together with a set of syntactical rules. 'Sentences' were composed of a sequence of words which expressed a unique semantic proposition and ranged in length from two to five words. In English, word order may drastically alter meaning and this was the case also in the artificial dolphin languages. The language which Akeakamai was taught was produced by computer-controlled wave-form generators and consisted of short whistle-like sounds. Phoenix was trained to use a gestural 'language' composed of unique movements of her trainer's arms and hands. The vocabulary of these languages consisted of words which could easily be combined with other words to form meaning-ful sentences. With a comparatively small vocabulary hundreds of sentences could be produced. While some of the words were used for training purposes, others were set aside for the testing of the comprehension of novel sentences and syntactical forms. A sentence might be novel lexically in that while the syntactical pattern is fam-iliar, there are new lexical items (words). Alternatively, a syntacti-cally novel sentence is one where the words are familiar but a new sentence form is introduced for the first time. A sentence might be reversible syntactically: 'Take the frisbee to the surf board' or 'Take the surf board to the frisbee'. To find out whether the dolphins had constraints on their ability to use word-order information, Phoenix used an inverse grammar rule ('to surf board, frisbee take'), while Akeakamai used a more straightforward left-to-right grammar ('frisbee take to surf board').

Quite apart from examining the sentence processing abilities of dolphins, Herman and his co-workers were aiming at studying the cognitive capabilities of the dolphins. Complex information processing was, they claimed, in part a skill which could be improved by edu-cation. In a similar way, the full realisation of human potential is largely dependent upon long-term special education. Knowledge struc-tures are greatly enriched through education, which serves to ex-pand the ability to recognise and solve problems.

Box 4.1 shows the vocabulary which Phoenix (P) and Akeakamai (A) were able to comprehend. Where a word is followed by an initial A or P only that dolphin understands the word.

Summary and Conclusions

1. Herman and his co-workers claim that their study has demon-strated that dolphins can understand imperative sentences and that this understanding involves the use both of the semantic and the syntactic elements of language. Phoenix and Akeakamai used two different modes, acoustic and visual, and two different

BOX 4.1

Comprehension Vocabulary of Dolphins (Herman *et al.*, 1984)

Comprehension vocabulary of Phoenix (P) and Akeakamai (A); if only one dolphin understands a listed word it is followed by the initial of that dolphin

OBJECTS

Tank fixtures	*Relocatable objects*[a]	*Transferable objects*[b]
GATE (divides portion of tank; can be opened or shut) (P)	SPEAKER (underwater)	BALL
	WATER (jetted from hose)	HOOP
WINDOW (any of four underwater windows)[c]	PHOENIX (dolphin as object) (A)	PIPE (length of rigid plastic pipe)
PANEL (metal panel attached underwater to side of tank)(P)	AKEAKAMAI (dolphin as object) (P)	FISH (used as object or reward)
	NET[c, d]	PERSON (any body part or whole person in or out of water)
		FRISBEE
		SURFBOARD
		BASKET

ACTIONS

Take direct object only	*Take direct and indirect object*
TAIL-TOUCH (touch with flukes)	FETCH (take one named object to another named object)
PECTORAL-TOUCH (touch with pectoral fin)	
MOUTH (grasp with mouth)	IN[c, d] (place one named object in or on another named object)
(GO) OVER	
(GO) UNDER	
(GO) THRU	
TOSS (throw object using rostrum movement)	
SPIT (squirt water from mouth at object)	

AGENTS

PHOENIX or AKEAKAMAI (prefix for each sentence; calls dolphin named to her station; indicates to dolphins which is to receive fish reward)

MODIFIERS

RIGHT or LEFT (used before object name to refer to object at that position) (A)

SURFACE or BOTTOM (used before object name to refer to object at that location) (P)

OTHER

ERASE (used in place of action word to cancel the preceding words – requires

the dolphin to remain at station or to return immediately)
YES (used after correctly executed instruction)
NO (sometimes used after incorrectly executed instruction – can cause emotional
    behavior)

[a] Objects whose locations may be changed by trainers.
[b] Objects that may be moved by dolphins – all names represent classes of
objects with multiple exemplars.
[c] Added to Akeakamai's vocabulary after completion of the majority of testing
reported in data tables.
[d] Added to Phoenix's vocabulary after completion of the majority of testing
reported in data tables.

sets of rules, in relation to word order. Regarding semantics both dolphins found it easy to generalise from one example of a class to others which they had not previously met. Not only were they able to understand lexically novel sentences (ones which contained words which they had not previously met) but structurally novel ones as well. This understanding of structural innovation included the integration of linked action words (i.e. turning more than one command into an integrated response). What these dolphins were able to demonstrate was far more than a set of stimulus response chains as occurs with operant conditioning. There was more reliance upon the understanding of sets of recombinable lexical elements held together by syntactical rules than upon contingencies between stimulus, response and reward.

2. It was claimed that the dolphins' ability to understand that arbitrary symbols could be made to stand for real world objects encouraged researchers to look more creatively at natural communication among animals.

3. Special, intensive and protracted education was seen as having dramatically enhancing effects upon the dolphins' cognitive and knowledge structures. They became more capable, in a general sense, as a result of the training they received. This has profound implications for human formal education.

4. Herman's work with dolphins represents a radical departure from the language work with apes carried out by researchers such as the Gardners, Patterson and Savage-Rumbaugh in that it concentrates upon comprehension rather than production of language. McNeill (1970) outlined reasons for studying comprehension rather than production in humans in the following terms:

In comprehension the investigator knows what the input to the process is – it is the sentence comprehended. Thus when comprehension fails, the source of the trouble can be located. The same cannot be said of production. (McNeill, 1970, p. 11)

5. As regards Hockett's criteria for language, much of it seems to be geared to the production of language rather than its comprehension, but there was evidence for displacement and semanticity in some of these studies with dolphins. The dolphins certainly understood meaning, and they both searched for missing objects which had been referred to and 'reported' their absence using the NO symbol.

Parrot Talk

It has long been assumed that the ability of parrots and similar birds to mimic human speech is simply that, mimicry, and does not imply that they are capable of using language with any degree of understanding. But Irene Pepperberg (1983, 1987, 1990) has been conducting studies with an African grey parrot (*Psittacus erithracus*) for about ten years and the studies seem to indicate that there is a a degree of understanding behind the mimicry. She taught the parrot to make same/different judgements about the shape, colour and material of objects. She also provided some evidence that the parrot was capable of object classification according to concepts, that is to say he was able to make classifications of objects according to relatively abstract criteria which were not based upon any single perceptual feature. This process of conceptualisation lies at the back of much language as opposed to the mere imitation of sounds.

There has been a considerable amount of research into the vocal abilities of mimetic birds going back to the 1940s, but though the birds were trained to reproduce language sounds they could not attach meaning to the sounds they produced. Pepperberg and her students were able to devise a vocal code for her parrot Alex which enabled her to examine his cognitive capabilities. She has outlined three conditions which facilitate exceptional vocal learning:

1. The subject must have the capacity to produce the sounds of human language. It is on this that the Kelloggs and the Hayes found difficulty with apes and it is this which led the Gardners to use ASL.

2. The subject must have the cognitive capacity to recognise that human sounds have a functional significance at least equivalent to their own sounds.
3. The subject must be given contextual support to learn the human sounds.

The first two of these conditions Pepperberg found relatively easy to meet using the parrot Alex. He was a good mimic and found no difficulty in reproducing the sounds of English. He had natural cognitive abilities which suggested that he would be able to recognise parallels between the language system he was being taught and his own natural communication system. Piaget (1952), Vygotsky (1962), Bandura (1971) and Todt (1975) have described the kinds of contextual support which facilitate the transfer of knowledge acquired in one domain to another. A concept or behaviour may be more readily learned if it is functional. Piaget has suggested that functionality may play a part in **assimilation**. He has used this term to describe the way in which children take in information and fit it into their existing knowledge. The function that information serves for the individual affects the ease with which it is assimilated. Todt demonstrated that African grey parrots learned their vocalisation most easily in a context of social interaction. A technique was developed by which humans play the roles of a young parrot's peers. In the wild, parrots engage in complex vocal duets and juvenile parrots observe these. Todt was able to set up a laboratory situation in which the young parrots observed humans engaged in the types of vocal exchanges which were to be learned. This greatly facilitated and speeded up the learning of parts of these exchanges.

Model/Rival Training

Based upon this, Pepperberg and her students developed what she termed **Model/Rival Training (M/R)**. For instance, the parrot observed two human trainers handling objects in which the parrot has shown interest. One human (the trainer) shows the object to another human who acts as model for the bird's responses and rival for the trainer's attention. The trainer asks the model/rival questions about the object(s) and rewards correct responses with praise and the object itself. Box 4.2 shows an excerpt from a Model/Rival training session.

BOX 4.2

M/R Training Used With Parrot, Alex (Pepperberg, 1983)

Excerpt From M/R Training Session, April 30, 1979

I: Kim, what color? (Holds up a green triangular piece of wood)

K: Green three-corner wood.

I: (Briefly removes object from sight, turns body slightly away). No! Listen! I just want to know color! (Faces back toward K; re-presents object) What *color*?

K: Green wood.

I: (Hands over exemplar) That's right, the color is *green*; green wood.

K: OK, Alex, now you tell me, what shape?

A: No.

K: OK, Irene, *you* tell me what shape.

I: Three-corner wood.

K: That's right, you listened! The shape is three-corner; it's *three-corner* wood (Hands over exemplar).

I: Alex, here's your chance. What color?

A: Wood.

I: That's right, wood; what *color* wood?

A: Green wood.

I: Good parrot! Here you go (Hands over exemplar). The color is green.

Note: I refers to the principal trainer, K to Kimberley Goodrich, one of the secondary trainers, and A to the parrot, Alex. This segment of the session lasted about 5 min.

These techniques have had significantly greater success in developing communication skills than have programmes of operant conditioning such as have been used in some of the ape studies (e.g. the Gardners and Washoe). On some occasions, when Alex had earned his reward he was able to reject the object about which the questions had been asked and correctly answered and to specify something else. However, his trainers would not respond to any such request as 'I want key' until a reward had been earned by successfully completing a task.

Avoidance of Unconscious Trainer Cueing

Terrace had criticised the Gardners' procedures (Terrace *et al.*, 1979) on the grounds that there was evidence of 'trainer cueing', albeit unconscious cueing, and Pepperberg has taken precautions against this possibility. For instance, neither the trainer nor Alex was able to predict the questions which would be asked on a particular day. The principal trainer would list all the possible questions about the objects to be presented. The student trainer who was administering the test then formed the questions and determined test order randomly. Test questions were then interspersed into training sessions on unrelated topics. The chance for any particular object to show up in a test might only occur once a week and so could not be predicted. No student who had trained Alex on a topic tested him on it as well.

Avoidance of Expectation Cueing

The intermingling of different types of question during tests or training on some other topic obviated expectation cueing. Alex was never tested successively in one session on similar questions. Only if the response was incorrect was the question repeated.

Scoring Procedures

To evaluate Alex's cognitive capacities on various tasks, test scores were arrived at. There were two ways of scoring:

1. The total of correct reponses was divided by the number of presentations required to arrive at an overall score.
2. Percentages of first correct trials (i.e where only one presentation was required) were arrived at for comparison.

Some Comparisons with Non-human Primates

The tasks on which Alex succeeded demanded a similar level of abstract information processing to those given to non-human primates such as Premack's Sarah. On a same/different task, for instance, he had to:

1. Pay attention to multiple aspects of two different objects.
2. Determine from a question posed vocally whether the response demanded an assessment of similarity or one of difference.
3. Determine which attribute was 'same' or 'different'.
4. Produce vocally a label for the category which represented this attribute.

Language Behaviour of an African Grey Parrot

Pepperberg has claimed her prime purpose to be the examination of Alex's cognitive capabilities rather than his language competence. She did not, unlike Herman's study described earlier, focus upon syntax (e.g. word order). Alex was not trained to use his communication code for self-reference, to express emotions or to attribute intentions to others. While Herman and his co-workers tested their dolphins using commands to which the correct response was compliance, Pepperberg used questions to elicit the production of vocal responses. Some of these vocalisations, acquired during training, were later heard used in *private* monologue speech. This is similar to behaviour observed in young children in the early stages of language acquisition. Pepperberg justifies this limitation of the scope of her investigation by the assertion that to examine linguistic competence *per se* would perhaps muddy the waters when the prime object is to examine the parrot's cognitive abilities.

As it relates to Hockett's criteria for language the above limitation makes assessment difficult. Like Herman, Pepperberg has claimed that the language training Alex received has enhanced his cognitive abilities. Concepts can be learned which Alex would otherwise have been unable to learn. She suggests, however, that training affects the ease with which learning can occur more than whether it can occur at all.

Self-Assessment Questions

1. What are the defining features of language, described by Hockett, which are relevant to whether apes can be said to be capable of learning language?
2. Describe two unsuccessful attempts made to teach apes to talk.
3. Discuss some of the attempts to teach apes non-vocal forms of language.

4. How does the work of Herman and his colleagues with dolphins and Pepperberg with an African grey parrot enhance our understanding of the nature of language?
5. Make some assessment of how far you think it right to say that language is no longer to be regarded as a species specific capacity of humans alone.

FURTHER READING

L. M. Herman (ed.), *Cetacean Behavior: Mechanisms and Functions* (New York: Wiley Inter-Science, 1980).

I. M. Pepperberg, 'Conceptual abilities of some non-primate species with an emphasis on an African Grey parrot', in S. T. Parker and K. Gibson (eds), *Language and Intelligence in Monkeys and Apes*: *Comparative Development Perspectives* (Cambridge: Cambridge University Press, 1990).

S. E. G. Lea, *Instinct, Environment and Behaviour* (London: Methuen, 1984).

E. O. Wilson, *Sociobiology: The New Synthesis* (Cambridge, Mass.: Harvard University Press, 1975).

A. Manning and M. Stamp Dawkins, *Animal Behaviour* (Cambridge: Cambridge University Press, 1992).

Social Behaviour 5

At the end of this chapter you should be able to:

1. Demonstrate ways in which animals' social grouping has advantages in relation to their survival.
2. Show what evolutionary functions follow from social behaviour of animals.
3. Describe the social organisation among insects such as honeybees and termites.
4. Describe and comment upon the forms of social organisation among primates.
5. Show some understanding of conflict behaviour, its origins and manifestations (e.g. territorial conflict, threat displays, appeasement and displacement behaviour).
6. Demonstrate an understanding of courtship, mating and parenting behaviours.

INTRODUCTION

One of the most striking features of all animals – and this includes humans – is their tendency to be social. This social behaviour can take various forms. Sometimes animals exist in pairs, sometimes in larger groupings, flocks, herds or schools. This chapter sets out to show how these forms of **social organisation** can be the result of natural selection and the genes that individual animals carry. It can be an advantage to a species to group together with others. Animals which carry genes which tend to make them interact with others in particular ways will in the right circumstances have an advantage and the genes they carry will be passed on.

SECTION I   FORMS OF SOCIAL ORGANISATION

By social organisation we are referring to the ways in which individual members of a species interact with each other. Some forms of social organisation will be rigid and species specific – among social insects, for instance – while others will be much more fluid, dynamic and dependent upon prevailing conditions. The diversity of forms of social organisation will include its permanence as well the purposes for which it exists. These social groupings include:

- **Societies**. These can be described as extremely stable relationships where individuals live in the same group for prolonged periods. Female elephants may live in the same family for 40 or 50 years.
- **Flocks of birds or schools of fish**. These are less complex and less durable forms of organisation. Individual birds, however, or fish may stay together for some months.
- **Aggregations**. These are the least permanent and durable forms of social organisation. Most commonly, aggregations occur when large numbers of members of a species gather at a common food source. Fruit flies, for instance, aggregate on a piece of rotten fruit. They are attracted to a common food source. Even here, though, there is some social organisation in that they react to each other, spacing themselves out so that they do not touch one another. Among humans you can see the way in which certain rules of aggregation are adhered to when large numbers of people come together. Even in a crowded street they will go to some lengths to prevent contact, stepping off the pavement into the road, for instance. Morris (1978) describes this maintenance of personal space:

> If a man enters a waiting room and sits at one end of a long row of chairs it is possible to predict where the next man to enter will seat himself. He will not sit next to the first man, nor will he sit at the far end, right away from him. He will choose a position about halfway between these points. The next man to enter will take the largest gap left and sit roughly in the middle of that and so on. . . . (Morris, 1978, p. 130)

Advantages of Grouping

Individuals who group themselves together do so because they are likely to be better off than they would be on their own. Better off implies being better adapted, more able to survive and pass on their genes. They have been said to be **fitter.** There are three ways in which we can discover what the advantages amount to:

1. We can use experimental methods. Some members of a species may be separated so that they are on their own, while others remain together. We can then observe how well the separate individuals and the groups succeed.
2. We can observe naturally occurring variations within a given species, those that group or those that do not.
3. Comparisons can also be made between species that are naturally solitary and those which are social.

It is also possible to argue from a purely theoretical standpoint, as Hamilton does in his 'Geometry for the Selfish Herd' (1971), that grouping together is inevitable. He has shown that if each individual animal tries to place at least one other animal between itself and a potential predator, the result will be tight groupings.

At a very basic level, Allee (1938) set out to discover the benefits gained by individuals even in loose aggregations. Water-fleas cannot survive in alkaline water. The respiration of a large number of them together was sufficient to make the water acid enough for them to survive. While individuals alone perished, groups survived.

Flocks of birds or schools of fish provide the following advantages for their members:

1. **Physical advantage**. Emperor penguins huddle close together against the cold as they incubate their eggs in the Antarctic winter. Thus the available heat is conserved and the outside penguins move more than those in the centre so that heat is generated in that way.

2. **Protection against predation**. Lazarus (1979) compared the responses of red-billed weaver birds to a predatory goshawk alone and in flocks with other birds. While the solitary birds failed to make any response at all, those in groups were much more likely to spot the predator. Using a hawk model, starlings were found by

Powell (1974) to spend much more of their time in surveillance and a much smaller amount of their time feeding when they were on their own than when they were in groups of ten or more. This finding is echoed by Elgar's (1989) review of more than 50 studies of both birds and mammals. The bigger the groups they are in, the greater proportion of their time they are able to spend feeding. Macdonald (1986) studied the habits of meerkats (*Suricatta suricatta*) which post lookouts while the rest of the group feeds.

3. **Defence against attack**. Predators have been found to be very reluctant to attack a group but instead to adopt the stratagem of attempting to make them scatter so that they can then single out isolated individuals (Hamilton, 1971). Göttmark and Andersson (1984) showed that gulls have much greater success in warding off predators in large groups than singly or in small groups. They band together to mob the predator.

4. **Better utilisation of food resources** represents a further advantage of group living. Sources of food found by one member of the group may be exploited by the group as a whole. Brown (1986) found that when individual cliff swallows had located a rich source of insect food they were followed on their next foray by less-successful members of the group. The original finders were not put at a disadvantage by this because the cache of food was so plentiful. Gannets are frequently found fishing in groups. Nelson (1980) suggested that the reason for this was that the fish become disorientated by the birds diving at them together and so are more easily caught.

5. **Facilitation of sexual activity**. The presence of other birds of the same species has the effect of stimulating sexual activity. This has been termed the **Fraser Darling** effect after the research of Fraser Darling:

> Though the immediate mate of the opposite sex may be the most potent excitatory individual to reproductive condition, other birds of the same species, or even similar species, may play a decisive part if they are gregarious at the breeding season. Without the presence of others the individual pairs of birds may not complete the reproductive cycle to the limit of rearing young to the fledgling stage. (Darling, 1938)

Smaller colonies of herring gulls start laying eggs at a later date and have a longer breeding season than large colonies. Consequently they are more exposed to predation by enemies. Darling claimed that in larger colonies the breeding season was shorter owing to social facilitation. The fact of social living makes breeding easier. Breeding is compressed into a shorter period of time when most other birds are also producing chicks. Predators are likely to be well fed at this time (with plenty of prey about) and they will be more likely to ignore individual chicks than they would be if they confronted a breeding pair on its own. Any particular chick therefore has a greater chance of survival.

6. **Group hunting among predatory species.** Among mammals a number of predatory species (for example, lions, hyaenas and hunting dogs) hunt in groups. They may drive their prey towards others hidden under cover or take turns to run their quarry to the point of exhaustion. Kruuk (1972) has described how the size of a pack of hyaenas hunting their prey will vary with the size of their quarry. Hunting zebra, the mean number of hyaenas in a group is 10.8, hunting adult wildebeest it is 2.5 and young gazelle fawns 1.2. When they are in an inappropriate sized group they ignore prey which in other circumstances they would attack.

Packer has suggested that the motives in this kind of group hunting are not entirely co-operative (Packer, 1986). The advantage lions gain in hunting together lies in being better able to protect the kill from scavengers and thieves rather than in making the kill in the first place.

A review of the literature by Martinez and Klinghammer (1970) has indicated that among marine mammals, killer whales (*Orcinus orca*) hunt in packs for sea-lions, whales and other dolphins.

But group living has costs as well. These include:

- **Competition for food**: Living in a group will inevitably mean that individuals will have to compete for food.
- **Disease**: The risk of transmission is likely to be greater.
- **Cannibalism**: Where the young are crowded together, there is some risk to the young from their own species.

As in many situations a balance needs to be struck in terms of survival. If the benefits of group living, which have been mentioned, outweigh the costs in terms of the individual animals surviving to pass on their genes, then social living traits will prevail at the expense of the genes which determine that animals live alone.

Hoogland and Sherman (1976) have listed a number of disadvantages which face bank swallows as a result of their communal nesting. There is greater risk, for instance, of their picking up fleas. There is also a greater likelihood of the burrow's collapsing because of large numbers of other birds nesting in it. However, it does appear that the advantages of communal living outweigh the potential risk.

Caste Systems Among Social Insects

While some insects lead what are perhaps the most solitary lives of all (the mason wasp, for instance, has contact with members of its species only for the briefest of periods during mating), some ants, bees and wasps have evolved complex social relationships which can be termed **caste** systems. Individuals are divided into workers, soldiers and reproductives. The members of each caste not only have quite discrete functions or roles within their group but have evolved anatomical differences as well. Wilson (1971) has described in some detail the social divisions within these colonies of social insects. He has defined the traits such insects exhibit as **eusocial.** Eusociality is defined by the common possession of three characteristics:

1. Co-operation among individuals of the same species in caring for the young.
2. Division of labour in reproduction. Sterile workers support fecund nestmates.
3. An overlap of at least two generations of life stages. Offspring will contribute to the support of their parents during some period of their life.

Determinants of Caste

1. Nutrition   It is interesting that the caste of an individual insect is determined as much by what it is fed on, as by any genetic determinant. Potentially, larval bees are all equal. Most get a restricted diet and develop into workers. Reproductive classes have an enriched diet.

2. Pheromones   Pheromones (chemical signals released into the air) are secreted by the insects themselves and co-ordinate development and social behaviour. A queen bee produces pheromones which suppress the reproductive capabilities of the workers. The supply of pheromenes has to be maintained. Where a honey-bee colony loses its queen the behaviour of some of the workers in the brood area begins to change. Emergency queen cells begin to be constructed, and some of the youngest workers begin to be fed royal jelly and are destined to become queens. Where queen substance falls below a critical level (through dilution as the size of the colony grows) there is a greater likelihood of swarming, which is the main means whereby new colonies are formed. Among honey-bees a single queen founds a colony, constructing the nest and rearing the first batch of workers. Then the workers take over foraging and extending the colony while the queen remains in the nest laying eggs.

Tasks Within Caste Systems

These are rigidly differentiated. Among honey-bees, workers have the following duties:

- Foraging
- Rearing the young
- Nest construction
- Attending the queen
- Guarding the colony

Among termite or ant colonies there are similar duties for the workers except there is sometimes an additional caste of 'soldier'. Soldiers have the sole function of guarding the colony. These develop enlarged jaws and other weapons. Function is very closely linked to nutrition. The functions of queens and other castes within the colony are also carefully defined. A relatively simple set of responses to particular stimuli enable the insects to have control over their environments and successfully adapt to them. There is a carefully evolved system of responses with limited flexibility. This is adaptiveness rather than intelligence.

Self-Assessment Questions

1. What are some of the forms of social grouping among animals? List the characteristics of each.
2. Explain some of the advantages and disadvantages of social grouping.
3. Describe the caste system of social organisation among insects. In what way does this system seem to you to have evolutionary advantages for the species concerned?

SECTION II   TERRITORY AND SOCIAL ORGANISATION

Defence of territory is important in the social organisation of many vertebrates. Territoriality represents a way in which animals can minimise competition for food, mates and nesting sites. Some animals are territorial during some parts of the year and gregarious at others. Great-tits vigorously defend territory during the nesting season, which means that at this important season they have an assured food supply, while in the winter they join together in large flocks, the better to locate scarcer food resources and protect them against predators. Defending a territory is not without its costs.

Economic Defendability of Territory

Brown (1969) has introduced the notion of **economic defendability**. Whether an animal will defend its territory will be determined by the value of the resources within it and whether it can be defended without the expense of too much energy. This idea of economic defendability has been examined by Gill and Wolf (1975). Nectar-feeding sunbirds in East Africa defend their territory vigorously against intruders. Gill and Wolf calculated the energy they expended defending this territory and matched it against the increased levels of nectar available to them in their 'private' flowers. They found territorial defence to be a very worthwhile use of energy.

Forms of Territorial Organisation

1. **The lek**. This is found in some species of grouse and other birds and in a few mammals. Males gather in a tight group or **lek** . Within this lek each male defends a small territory of his own. The sight of so many males displaying together lures females from far and wide who come and choose their mates on the basis of this fashion parade. Henley or Ascot might be seen also as a similar 'marriage market' for the human species. Gibson and Bradbury (1985) have shown that among grouse the males who display for the longest time and the most vigorously are most likely to be chosen by females. The sole purpose of this lek area seems to be that of a marriage market, because the females once mated go off on their own to raise their young. The males offer them no assistance at all but continue to attract other females.

2. **Nest sites**. Pied fly-catchers have a different use of territory. Males arrive about a week ahead of females at breeding grounds in Northern Europe, beginning with the oldest males with the blackest plumage. These birds have the pick of the best territories. The success they have in attracting a mate could be due to either of the following factors:

- That they have the best sites.
- That they are individually the most attractive. Black is clearly beautiful.

An ingenious experiment by Alatalo *et al.* (1986) aimed to separate the above two factors. Pied fly-catchers will regularly nest in artificial nest boxes. The researchers restricted the number of available nest boxes available at any one time, only putting up more when the first were occupied. When the females arrived, the researchers carefully noted the order in which the males found a mate. They found that it was the quality of the territory which was most attractive to the females rather than individual characteristics such as age or blackness of plumage. In terms of fitness this makes excellent sense. The survival of the brood is more dependent on cover and food supply than upon handsomeness of plumage or age. It seems more important for the bride that the bridegroom should be well endowed with this world's goods than that he should be handsome! The 'sexy son' hypothesis also has received some attention. This involves females choosing handsome sons because their sons will also be handsome and so will find it easier to find a mates.

Territory, Social Organisation and Mating Behaviour

There is an established relationship between the type of social or territorial organisation of members of a species and the mating system adopted (i.e. the relationships and roles of the two sexes in reproduction). Factors include the following.

1. Mating Systems and Territory

Where there are 'lek' type territories animals tend to be polygamous, while animals which have to defend large territories are either monogamous or have just 2 or 3 females to each male. Jarman (1974) found inter-relationship between diet, territory, body size and mating system in different species of antelope. With smaller antelope, duikers or dik-dik for instance, the male lives with a single mate in a territory which he defends to provide food for her and their offspring throughout the year. Larger antelopes, gazelles, waterbuck and impala have a social organisation involving large groups, ranging from 6 to 100-plus animals. They do not stay in the same area all year but males defend territories vigorously against other males and attempt to mate with any females entering it. Males are promiscuous, mating with as many females as possible as they enter their territory, while females wander from territory to territory in search of food, mating as they go.

2. Access to Potential Mate

A factor which determines the kind of social organisation of a given species may be the control of access by others to potential mates. Emlen and Oring (1977) have shown that polygamy may evolve where males defend a group of females to provide them with the food they need.

3. Scarcity of Food Resources

Crook (1965) has suggested that there is a relationship between the scarcity or otherwise of food resources and the mating system adopted. Among weaver birds, forest species are solitary nesters, monogamous and insectivorous; savannah species on the other hand nest in colonies, eat seeds and are polygynous (that is, one male to several females). Monogamy seems to be favoured when there is scarcity of food, polygyny when it is plentiful. In the latter case it does not seem to be so essential that there should be a male at hand for each female to help with the rearing of the brood. However, Crook's conclusions have not been universally accepted. Haartman (1969) has suggested other factors which could have an effect upon mating sytems – the kind of nest sites available, for instance. In any case , Crook's findings with weaver birds do not seem to hold with other species. There is some further definition of terms used on p. 179.

4. Survival Chances of the Young

The mating system adopted will be that which provides the greatest chance for the young of the species to survive. The need for both parents to be at hand to feed and care for the young indicates that monogamy is desirable, while in cases where one parent is quite capable of rearing the young on her own polygyny offers the chance for the male to pass on his genes to a larger number of offspring. Polygyny or promiscuity are the most common mating systems among mammals except where the male makes a substantial contribution to the upbringing of the young. With birds, things are different. Incubation demands the attention of both parents, as does the collection of food for the young, so a high proportion of bird species are monogamous.

The Polygyny Threshold Model

A model has been developed by Verner and Wilson (1966) and Orians (1969) which has become known as the **polygyny threshold model,** which relates the need for the male to care for the brood to the desirability (from the male's point of view) of having several families and so pass on his genes to more offspring. It may pay a female, too, to settle for a lower level of care for the brood by the male in return for a higher quality of territory, rather than mate monogamously with a male who only has a poor territory. On good territory a female may have better success in raising her brood, in spite of the competition of other females, providing there are not too many of them. Beyond a certain threshold of numbers, she might do better in a monogamous mating on poorer territory.

However, Davies (1989) has pointed out that the model does not always fit the data. What is best for males may not always be what is best for females. The mating system which evolves may be a compromise. Catchpole *et al.* (1985) showed that among great reed warblers where migrating females arrive later than the males, the fine characteristics of a particular male's territory may occasionally attract several females to settle there. The polygyny threshold model would suggest that their breeding success ought to be at least as good as that of monogamous birds on poorer territory. But it does not happen like that. The later arrivals do significantly less well. The males benefit, but the females are worse off than if they had a single unmated male on a poorer territory.

Contributions Made by Males

The contribution made by males of a given species to the upbringing of the brood is correlated with differences between the sexes in their appearance and displays. In species in which the male mates many times but contributes nothing to the brood except his sperm there are the greatest differences in size and appearance between the sexes. A peahen is a very dowdy creature in comparison with the magificent plumage of the peacock. His courtship ritual is spectacular but he does not care for his young at all. Male elephant seals are some three or four times the size of the female, but the responsibility for raising the pups rests entirely with the female. Intense competition between the males of such species as elephant seals and red deer allows the female to choose that male which is likely to contribute the best (i.e. the most well-adapted) genes (his sole contribution), and the successful competitor can then assemble a large entourage of females. Among elephant seals, in some seasons as few as 4 per cent of the males are responsible for 85 per cent of the matings (Le Boeuf, 1974). Such males are very successful in passing on their genes and here again the 'sexy son' phenomenon operates. Females choose the 'likeliest lads' to father their offspring in the expectation of handsome offspring who will find no difficulty in attracting females.

Self-Assessment Questions

1. What are some of the advantages of territoriality in terms of evolutionary success?
2. What is meant by a lek? What are the characteristics of lek type organisation?
3. What relationship seems to exist between scarcity or otherwise of resources and mating systems among animals?
4. Among species where polygyny is the norm there is often great disparity between the sexes. Can you identify an evolutionary reason for this?

SECTION III   SOCIAL DOMINANCE

As long ago as 1935, Schelderup-Ebbe developed notions of **social dominance hierarchies**. He observed 'pecking orders' among flocks of hens. In any flock there emerged one who was dominant and could displace all others. Below her was a second bird who was able to displace all but the first, and so on until at the bottom of the hierarchy was a bird displaced by all. This is an alternative form of social organisation to territoriality but not clearly distinguished from it. Animals cannot be categorised as either territorial or hierarchical. For some the social system is seasonal. Fraser Darling's account of the social organisation of red deer (1935), and Clutton-Brock and Albon's (1989) more recent study of this species on Rhum in the Hebrides, showed that outside the breeding season males and females live apart. Among males there is a clear linear social dominance hierarchy. The larger stags become dominant and are able to displace the smaller ones, lower placed in the hierarchy, from the best feeding spots. Hierarchy does not have the same importance among hinds. The pattern changes in the rutting season, though. Males go off singly to display areas and roar to attract hinds. The stags then defend the group of females they have collected during the few weeks of the rutting season. Thereafter they return to their former separate herds.

Social Organisation Among Primates

Because humans are themselves primates there has been great interest in the way in which primates organise themselves socially. The majority of primates are social animals with relatively stable and cohesive social groups. Jolly (1966) in her study of ring-tailed lemurs (*Lemur catta*) showed them to move around in troops of around 12–20 animals which included both adult males and breeding females. They are also territorial. Troops occupy territories marked by scent. Mothers and infants have close contact with each other, and as the infants grow older other adults approach and play with them as well. This seems to characterise a typical primate organisation. In human families the closest contact in the initial period after birth is between mother and child. Other adults play an increasing role as the child grows older. Between species, the size of troops varies widely, from baboons whose troops are sometimes very large to almost solitary orang-utans.

Inter-Communication Among Primates

A feature of primate social organisation is the way in which individuals within a group are constantly attentive to other members of the group. Posture, gestures, movements and calls all provide means of communication and responses to each other. Primate groups are highly complex for a number of reasons:

- **Long infant dependency.** There is a long period in their life cycle during which the young are dependent.
- **Longevity.** Larger species of primates can live for 20–30 years and humans much longer than that. Within a group, therefore, every individual is likely to know every other individual from long experience.
- **Intelligence.** Primates are intelligent animals with high levels of learning ability. As the social situation within a group changes, the responses each individual makes to that situation are highly flexible. Humphrey (1976) has suggested that it is the complex demands of the the primates' social life which has led through evolutionary selection to growth in the size of primate brains, and in turn the growth in brain size offered greater flexibility and complexity in their relations with each other. The apotheosis of

this development is, of course, the human brain. Gene-culture co-evolution described, in some detail in Chapter 1 is a major contributor to the phenomenal development of the human species.

Dominance and subordination are important features of the social relationships among primates. As with other species, dominance involves the threat of displacement or even attack, though as rank becomes established it becomes increasingly less necessary to carry through threats or attacks. Grooming is an important manifestation of dominance. Dominant individuals allow themselves to be groomed by a subordinate as a placatory gesture. Sexual presentation is also used as an appeasement gesture. Among baboons and chimpanzees it is a frequent response to a threatening and dominant animal. Having a high rank within a group implies that a dominant individual's behaviour is not limited by other individuals. In all species, including humans, high-ranking, dominant individuals have greater freedom to act than low-ranking, subordinate ones. Choice is not for all equally, but is greater for dominant individuals. In almost all primate groups there seems to be a hierarchy of rank which determines the behaviour of individuals.

Rowell (1974), however, has disputed this analysis. She has suggested that dominance hierarchies are largely the result of the crowding and unnatural stress which exists among *captive* groups. Dominance hierarchies, she found, are not common among wild groups of primates, and where they do exist are more a matter of deference by subordinates than aggression by the dominant. Displays of threat are less common than displays of deference. When obvious evidence of dominance hierarchies existing in the wild has been shown it could be the result in part of human interference. Goodall (1968) found that when she placed caches of food for her chimpanzees, the dominant males sat in the best places and the rest of the group spaced out according to rank. Where the food had to be searched for individually, the influence of rank was less obtrusive. Others, however, have found clear evidence of hierarchies in wild and undisturbed primate colonies. Deag (1977), for instance, found a linear hierarchy among a troop of Barbary macaques.

Survival Functions of Hierarchies

Hierarchies of this kind have an important survival function. There are clear advantages, not only for high-ranking but for low-ranking individuals. They include the following:

- **Cohesion**. It is vital for the survival of all the members of a troop that it should stay together.
- **Predictability of social interactions.** It is to the benefit of all members of the troop, not only of the high but of the low rankers as well, that they should be able to predict how other members of the troop will react to them.
- **Avoidance of stress.** There is likely to be less fighting and stress when the outcome of conflicts can be predicted in advance. Less favoured animals will be likely to keep clear of those to whom they will inevitably lose in any competition.
- **Fluidity of hierarchies.** Rankings are not fixed for all time. As circumstances change and dominant animals become older, subordinate animals will take over.

Primate social structures are complex, however, and hierarchies may not always be linear. Studies by van der Waal (1989) in Arnhem Zoo, of free-ranging rhesus monkeys on Cayo Santiago Island (Colvin, 1983) and of African vervet monkeys (Cheney, 1983) show dynamic structures, with alliances formed, broken up and re-formed among individual animals.

Dominance and Sex

Males frequently breed outside the group in which they were born but females tend to remain in the group along with mothers and sisters. For males, their rank in a group is largely determined by size. As they become sexually mature they frequently leave the group into which they were born and this results from disputes over dominance. With females the hierachy is different. The rank the mother holds determines the position of her daughters, the youngest mature daughter ranking immediately behind the matriarch with her sisters in reverse order of age. Gouzoules and Gouzoules (1987) have demonstrated that this is evolutionarily sensible. The youngest daughter gets most support from her mother because she has the longest reproductive span ahead of her and so has the greatest chance of passing on her genes – that is, once she has surmounted the perils of infancy and come to maturity.

Permanence of relationships between the sexes varies between species. In those just discussed, several adult males and adult females live together with no permanent male–female bonds. In other species, the family group tends to consist of just one adult male, a harem of females and their offspring. The surplus males form all-male troops, whose members occasionally challenge a male in a family group. Kummer's studies with hamadryas baboons give insight into these relationships (Kummer, 1968; Bachmann and Kummer, 1980). Baboons were caught from the wild and set up in cages. Where two unattached males were caged together and a female introduced, threats and sometimes fighting ensued until the female became attached to one of the males (usually the dominant one). Sometimes, the subordinate male was first caged singly with the female who was allowed to interact and pair with him. Then when they were put all together, the dominant male made no overtures at all to the female, if she were strongly paired already to the other male. There seemed to be the same social inhibition against poaching someone else's girl as is evident in human society.

Self-Assessment Questions

1. What is the meaning of the term 'social dominance hierarchy'?
2. What evidence is there of social dominance hierarchies among primate species?
3. In what ways are the social relationships of primates more complex than among other species? Can you account for this complexity?
4. What evidence is there for there being a relationship between the sex of primates and dominance?

SECTION IV PARENTS AND OFFSPRING

The previous sections of this chapter have alluded to the relationships between the upbringing of offspring and patterns of social and sexual relationships. This section aims to tie up some loose ends. There are various questions to be considered:

- What means are employed to ensure that members of a species find the most evolutionarily advantageous mating system?. In other words, how does sexual selection operate?
- To what extent are interactions between parents and offspring governed by natural selection?
- What evolutionary role is played by imprinting and other forms of bonding between adults and young?
- How does this tie in with what is known about mother/infant interactions in the human species?
- What are the consequences of disturbance to parental care?

Sexual Selection

There needs to be a means whereby males and females of a species find each other and remain together long enough to copulate. This can pose quite a problem for species which are solitary or widely dispersed. What is more, the chances need to be high that the off-spring from copulation will be successfully reared. Females, which contribute not only genes but also some store of food in the 'ovum', need to be relatively sure that it is a male of the right species which copulates with her, so that her investment will not be wasted. Hybrids are infertile. As we have seen, visual displays such as that of the peacock, audible displays, as with the red deer, contribute to this insurance.

Promiscuity may be associated with female care for the young. Chimpanzee females only come into oestrus infrequently (maybe once in two years). Then all the males in the group will copulate with her. Care of the young is almost entirely in the hands of the females.

Theory of Parental Investment

Because of **anisogamy** (the fact that males and females do not have equal contributions to make, but female gametes accommodate the store of food mentioned above) females are virtually assured of finding a mate. Males on the other hand contribute relatively little. Consequently, it is in their interest to make their contribution in as many places as they can, to invest in as many females as they can. The exceptions are those species where the male makes a large contribution to the rearing of offspring. In these cases, the females have to compete for a mate. In a classic experiment Bateman (1948) documented the effects of anisogamy among fruit flies (*Drosophila melanogaster*). The flies had chromosomal markings which enabled Batemen to identify individuals. Groups of five males were introduced to five virgin females. Each female thus had five males to choose from and each female had to compete with four other rivals. Only 4 per cent of the females, but 21 per cent of males failed to find a mate. Even the unlucky 4 per cent of females were vigorously courted and most of the males repeatedly attempted to mate. In terms of success the most successful males produced almost three times as many offspring as the most successful females.

Trivers (1972) developed a **theory of parental investment**. According to this theory there is a relationship between parental investment (defined as any behaviour toward the offspring which increases the offspring's chances of survival) and reproductive success (the number of offspring surviving). The sex with the smaller per-offspring investment will have a greater variance in reproductive success and so there will be more competition among members of that sex. Consequently, greater intra-sexual display and more techniques of sexual selection will evolve. In most cases the sex with the greatest contribution to make towards raising offspring will be the female. But in some species the females are the more competitive sex. In those cases the females indulge in the most conspicuous display.

The male of a species which fertilises by insemination (and this includes all mammals, birds and reptiles) cannot be certain that the offspring which his mate is bringing up are in fact his own. It is to his advantage, from the point of view of passing on his genes, to have exclusive access to the unfertilised eggs of the female. There are various ways in which this exclusivity can be brought about:

1. Dominance systems are one way of avoiding sperm competition. The dominant male will have first access to the available females.
2. In monogamous birds exclusivity is ensured by a time lag between bonding and copulation. This acts as a quarantine period to allow alien sperm to be detected. It is interesting to speculate whether betrothal serves the same purpose in human societies. Couples may become engaged as a preliminary bonding to ensure that there has been no adulteration prior to marriage.

Adulterers have had harsh treatment in many human societies. Among Eskimos, Australian Aborigines and Bushmen murder or fighting resulting in death usually seems to be the result of retaliation for actual or suspected adultery. In more sophisticated human societies there have been very harsh penalties meted out to females found to be adulterous – stoning, for example, among the Jews of Biblical times.

Another dimension has been added to the issue of sexual exclusivity (among humans, at least) by the introduction and use of DNA 'fingerprinting'. Short sequences of the DNA message are repeated within the double helix which forms the genetic blueprint in every organism. The number of times a sequence is repeated and the position in which these repeats occur are peculiar to a particular individual. DNA fingerprints are part of the genetic inheritance of each of us, and have been used by the agency that has been set up to track down fathers reluctant to pay proper maintenance for their children, the Child Protection Agency (CPA), to prove paternity in cases where an errant father has disputed his responsibilty. It is also used extensively in criminal cases as an alternative to actual fingerprints, because any single trace of DNA will suffice to provide the evidence, particularly in cases of rape where a trace of sperm will be sufficient to provide a DNA fingerprint. There is a full discussion of the issue of DNA fingerprinting in Jones (1993), *The Language of the Genes*. While it was at first supposed that this method of identification was as near to being infallible as it could be (in one American court the chance of being wrong on a DNA identification was described as one in seven hundred and thirty eight million million) it is not now considered to be quite so foolproof. Human beings are not infallible and there have been mistakes in labelling and also in the comparison by eye of the stained bands of each sample.

Courtship, then, has a betrothal role to play among animals, apart from its more obvious functions of ensuring choice of the right sex and species before copulation, overcoming aggression and arousing responsiveness in the partner.

Some Definitions

Wilson (1975) claims polygamy to be natural for all animals. Monogamy, where it occurs, is the result of evolutionary pressure to equalise the parental investment in the rearing of offspring. This forces the establishment of sexual bonds. The evidence for his claim depends to an extent on definition of terms. **Monogamy** implies that one male and one female join to rear at least one brood exclusively. Sometimes it extends for a lifetime. **Polygamy** covers any form of multiple mating. A form of polygamy where one male mates with several females is termed **polygyny.** The converse (where one female mates with several males) is **polyandry.** Polygamy may be serial or simultaneous: matings may take place in succession or more or less at the same time. Where simultaneous polygyny occurs it can be referred to as **harem polygyny.** In most cases there is at least a temporary **pair bond**, even in polygamous species. Where there is not this bond polygamy can be said to be **promiscuous.** Even in promiscuous relationships, according to Selander (1972), matings are not random but highly selective.

Wilson (1975) lists five general conditions which promote polygamy:

1. Local or seasonal superabundance of food.
2. Risk of heavy predation.
3. Precocial young.
4. Sexual bimaturism (males and females of some species come to maturity at different ages) and extended longevity.
5. Nested territories due to niche division between the sexes.

Much of the details of the above conditions have been mentioned earlier in this chapter, but it is appropriate to summarise here.

Superabundance of Food

The condition of **superabundance of food** relates to the **polygyny threshold** model of Orians (1969) and Verner (1965) (sometimes termed the Orians–Verner model). This links polygyny to the availability of easy food resources, or conversely, monogamy to comparative scarcity.

Predation

Where there is **heavy predation** on a species there will be a greater chance of offspring being raised if both parents are there to provide protection. This favours monogamy. Von Haartman (1969) relates polygyny to the nest sites preferred by particular species. Where these are well protected males may spend more time courting additional females.

Precocial Young

In species which have **precocial young**, which can move around and fend for themselves very early, there is less need for male participation in the upbringing of offspring and they can devote more of their energies to display and to fighting for additional mates. Polygynous species with precocial young include pheasants, partridges and the like, but the relationship between precocity in the young and polygyny is certainly not invariable. Exceptions include swans, geese and ducks.

Sexual Bimaturism and Extended Longevity

Sexual bimaturism refers to the fact that in some species males and females mature at different ages. Among these and among long-lived species there is a tendency to defer reproduction until they are large amd mature enough to gain dominance. During their first year adults do not mate, though females breed freely in the first year. The dominance gained by this forbearance leads to the insemination of more than sufficient females to make up for the loss during the first year. Bimaturism is widespread among polygynous species of birds and mammals. Examples include elephant seals (*Mirounga leonina*) (Carrick *et al.*, 1962), mountain sheep (Geist, 1971) and red-winged blackbirds (Peek, 1971).

Nested Territories

Where species breed within the confines of a feeding territory and the female is smaller than the male (or for some other reason requires less space) and if she cares for her offspring on her own, a given feeding territory will be able to support more than one female. Thus lizards (*Anolis*) and geckos (*Gehyra variegata*) have evolved polygamous mating behaviour (Schoener and Schoener, 1971; Bustard, 1970).

Instinctive Mechanisms of Care

The important thing is that the offspring should survive to reach adulthood. In many instances this means that some parental care is necessary. The very young have not had the time to learn what they have to do to be cared for from experience, so that much of their behaviour must be instinctive. There is instinctive behaviour on both sides of the interaction between adult and young as the following examples show:

- Parent herring gulls are instinctively ready to open their beaks to regurgitate food when chicks peck at them (Tinbergen and Perdeck, 1950).
- A comparison has been made between the feeding rituals of razor bills and guillemots. While the guillemot parent presents the chicks with a single fish tail first, sheltering the fish at the same time with its wings and feet, the razor bill presents the fish in its bill openly for the young to peck at. Each species evolved ritual instinctive behaviour with which to ensure the survival of their own chicks. When eggs were transferred from the nest of one species to that of the other many of the chicks died before they could adapt to the foreign feeding rituals of the other species. Parents and offspring in either case had mutually adapted to the responses of their own young.

Trevarthen (1975) has investigated the interactions of human babies with adults. He coined the term 'pre-speech' to describe the mouth movements he observed during these interactions. He suggested that babies were endowed at birth with quite complex abilities. Similarly Condon and Sander (1974) analysing video recordings of babies' interactions with their caregivers reported that they appeared to synchronise their movements to the rhythms of the speech of adults. This synchrony they saw as the prototype of the turn-taking which is part of adult conversation.

Imprinting

The phenomenon of **imprinting**, described in Chapter 2, represents yet another set of interactions between offspring and adults. Environmental circumstances are clearly involved as well. Species which are able to move around as soon as they are born or hatched, such as ducklings or goslings, face the problem of the mutual recognition of parents and offspring. This can particularly prove a problem where animals live in groups. They need to make sure they are caring only for their own offspring. Imprinting is a rapid form of learning. The young animal is predisposed by instinct to respond to any object it sees or hears during a fairly short 'sensitive' period after hatching. Lorenz (1952) had grey-lag goslings follow him wherever he went, even into the lake to teach them to swim. Many imprinting experiments have been done which have shown young birds 'imprint' on many different bright, noisy moving objects.

Mechanisms of Attachment in Mammals

This kind of mechanism for mutual attachment of adults to offspring does not seem to be restricted to birds. Goats and sheep need to see and smell kids or lambs shortly after birth or they will reject them. Farmers attempting to make a sheep accept a lamb which does not belong to it sometimes impregnate the lamb with its foster-mother's smell by rubbing it with its bedding straw. The mechanism seems to be a matter of instinct, but it depends upon triggers in the environment to become operative.

Even in the case of humans, though we are not a species which is mobile at birth as birds and sheep or goats are, there still seem to be mechanisms which attach the baby to its mother at a very early stage. MacFarlane (1975) has shown that babies will respond selectively to their own mother's bra-pads as young as three days old and there is selective response to her voice by thirty days old (Mehler *et al.*, 1978).

Failure of Attachment

Harlow and Harlow (1965) claimed that young rhesus monkeys needed a strong attachment to adults if they were to grow up properly. Reared in isolation in laboratory conditions the monkeys then behaved strangely when adult. They were unable to mate normally and even when artificially inseminated the females could not care for their young. The substitution of a hard (wire) 'mother' did nothing to alleviate the problem even when supplied with a nipple, though a soft (towelling) mother did slightly reduce abnormal behaviour.

It was against this background that Bowlby (1953) formulated what became known as **the theory of maternal deprivation** with his book *Child Care and the Growth of Love*. His suggestion was that where a human child failed to have a proper attachment to his/ her mother in infancy behavioural development was likely to be impaired. Goodall (1974) in her observations of chimpanzees in Tanzania records the death of Flo, one of the chimpanzee mothers she was observing. Flo had a son, already eight years old and independent, but such was his depression following his mother's death that he stopped eating and died shortly afterwards. Among humans, too, bereavement is an important cause of illness and even death. Parkes (1972) has identified three stages of reaction to bereavement:

1. Denial, during which stage the bereaved person refuses to see the death as 'real'.
2. Pining which involves intense longing for the dead person, restlessness or even hallucinatory sightings of the deceased in a crowd or at a distance.
3. Depression which include feelings of apathy, self-blame and anguish.

There is some evidence that the attachment does not need to be with the mother or indeed with an adult at all. The Harlows (Harlow and Harlow, 1965) found that animals reared without their mothers but with other infant monkeys grew up into normal adults. Freud and Dann (1951) studied six 3-year-old orphans who had spent most of their lives together in a German concentration camp. They had had no mother or father figure, but had formed very close attachments to each other.

Among animals also, the care of the young does not come exclusively from the mother. Fathers also provide care, exclusively in the case of sticklebacks, partially in the cases of several kinds of monkey. Among titi and some marmosets males carry the infants most of the time when they are not actually feeding (Mitchell, 1964). In other species the mother provides most of the care for the first year but when there is a new infant born the father takes over, at least to some extent. Rowell *et al.* (1964) describe what they call 'aunting' among some troop living primates. Juvenile females who have not yet given birth themselves find any new-born animal of intense interest. They will pick the infant up, pass it round and even run off with it. The chances are that they will be related to the mother. If by taking over in this way they relieve the mother then they are increasing the chances of successful rearing of offspring to carry on the line. They are also giving themselves experience which will stand them in good stead when they come to raise their own infants.

Kin Selection

Kin selection is also a factor where birds such as moorhens lay more than one clutch of eggs in a season. In such cases the young of the first brood stay with their mother throughout the season and help feed the second brood which are, of course, their siblings. This relates to the discussion of altruism and kinship selection which is fully discussed in Chapter 1.

Evolutionary interests of Parents and Offspring

If we have taken as the theme the ways in which the genes may best be passed on, there is clearly a balance to be struck between the numbers of young produced and the care which is afforded to each one. A human being may produce two or perhaps three children and devote a great deal of care and attention to them, sometimes for the best part of twenty years. In the past, families produced more children, perhaps as many as fifteen or twenty, fully expecting that not all of them would survive, and this is still the case in less-developed societies. Similarly, among animal species it is not unknown for parents to stop feeding the weakest of a litter when times get hard, and even feed it to its siblings (Polis, 1981).

Trivers (1974) has suggested there is an apparent conflict of interest between parents and offspring. While the adults have an interest in dividing the available food resources fairly, so that all the offspring may have a good chance of surviving (notwithstanding the special case mentioned above), each individual offspring has an interest in getting as much as possible. While its siblings do share some of its genes, they do not share all of them. Altruism towards relatives has been discussed in Chapter 1.

Again there can be a conflict when the time comes for the offspring to become independent. In human terms, it is not infrequent to find adolescents lingering on in the protected environment of home, perhaps pursuing yet another course of study, just so long as the parents will fund it. So far as passing on the genes is concerned, he or she would be better off finding a mate and rearing a new family. But of course there is always the problem of finding the resources to be able to bring them up. Where animals produce young serially, one at a time, as is the case with cattle, for instance, there is a stage of conflict when the parent abandons the young animal which has now reached maturity, in favour of producing and caring for the next.

Much of the contents of the preceding paragraphs has juxtaposed human and animal behaviour to emphasise that to an extent we are all animals and much of animal behaviour has resonances for us too.

Some Conclusions

This chapter and the book as a whole takes a sociobiological approach to the behaviour of animals, and this includes humans. Natural selection is the guiding principle. This involves the way in which one allele (one of a pair of genes, each of which determines a particular sort of behaviour or characteristic) survives into the next generation because it is 'fitter' or better adapted than the alternative allele. But this is by no means the whole story. Culture and learning are important also. The culture and the environment in which a creature lives and its capacity for learning have a crucial impact upon its behaviour and its behaviour in turn will influence its chances of survival. Gene-culture co-evolution has been referred to in Chapter 1 and goes some way towards accounting for why humans have developed at a much faster rate than animal species.

The sociobiological approach has not been without its critics and some of the initial hostility towards the ideas it espouses have also been outlined in Chapter 1. Rose *et al.* (1990) castigates it as just another example of genetic determinism, ignoring other levels of explanation (e.g. social, cultural or cognitive explanations). However, Lumsden and Wilson (1983) have gone some way towards meeting this determinist criticism, as has been outlined in Chapter 1. Sociobiologists, additionally, are using the term 'gene' rather differently from the way in which it is used by geneticists. Dawkins (1976) refers to it as a 'unit of natural selection' without fully explaining the biological processes which go on in the cell. Hayes

(1986) has criticised this as being circular and misleading. Gould (1981) has also criticised the methodology employed by sociobiologists in trying to explain particular instances of animal behaviour in terms of their evolutionary significance, rather than endeavouring to discover the principles and mechanisms which underlie behaviour. Hinde (1987) has argued that while the biological perspective taken by the sociobiologists is important it is only one of several ways of explaining human behaviour. Extrapolating from animal to human behaviour is dangerous. Humans have different levels of cognitive ability from animals and have capacity for language. Animal species are also enormously diverse, as Wilson (1992) has demonstrated in his book *The Diversity of Life*. However, if this account provides insights into the behaviour of humans and animals then it will have served its purpose.

Self-Assessment Questions

1. What is the 'theory of parental investment'? How does it link parental investment in offspring with competition for sexual selection?
2. What are some of the ways in which interactions between adult and offspring are instinctive?
3. Attachment of young to adults is clearly important in a wide range of species. To what extent does it appear to be due to learning?
5. What sources of conflict of interest exist between parents and offspring?

FURTHER READING

A. Manning and M. Dawkins, *Animal Behaviour*, 4th edn (Cambridge: Cambridge University Press, 1992).

S. E. G. Lea, *Instinct, Environment and Behaviour* (London: Methuen, 1984).

Bibliography

Adams, D. B. (1986) 'Ventromedial tegmental lesions abolish offense without disturbing predation or defense', *Physiology and Behaviour*, 38, 165–8.

Adler, N. T. (1974) 'The behavioural control of reproductive behaviour', in W. Montague (ed.), *Reproductive Behaviour* (New York: Plenum Publishing Company).

Alatalo, R. V., Lundberg, A. and Glynn, C. (1986) 'Female pied fly-catchers choose territory quality not male characteristics', *Nature* (London).

Albert, D. J., Petrovic, D. M. and Walsh, M. L. (1989) 'Competitive experience activates testosterone-dependent social aggression towards unfamiliar males', *Physiology and Behavior*, 45, 225–8.

Allee, W. C. (1938) *The Social Life of Animals* (New York: Norton).

Altmann, S. A. (1962) 'The social behavior of anthropoid primates: analysis of recent concepts', in E. L. Bliss (ed.), *Roots of Behavior* (New York: Harper & Brothers).

Andersson, M. (1982) 'Sexual selection, natural selection and quality advertisement', *Biological Journal of the Linnaean Society*, 17, 375–9.

Andrew, R. J. (1985) 'The temporal structure of memory formation', *Perspectives in Ethology* (New York: Plenum Press), 6, 219–59.

Andrew, R. J. (ed.) (1991) *Neural and Behavioural Plasticity: The Use of the Domestic Chick as a Model* (Oxford and London: Oxford University Press).

Astington, J. W., Harris, P. L. and Olson, D. R. (1988) *Developing Theories of Mind* (Cambridge: Cambridge University Press).

Aston-Jones, G. and Bloom, F. (1981) 'Norepinephrine-containing locus coerulus neurons in behaving rats exhibit pronounced responses to nonnoxious environmental stimuli', *Journal of Neuroscience*, 1, 887–900.

Bachman, C. and Kummer, N. (1980) 'Male arrangement of female choice in hamadryas baboons', *Behavioural Ecological Sociobiology*, 6, 315–21.

Baddeley, A. (1990) *Human Memory* (Hove, East Sussex: Lawrence Erlbaum Associates Ltd).

Baerends, G. P. (1957) 'The ethological concept "releasing mechanism" illustrated by a study of the stimuli eliciting egg-retrieving in the herring gull', *Anatomical Record*, 128, 518–19.

Baerends, G. P. (1959) 'The value of the concept "releasing mechanism"', *Proceedings of the XVth International Congress of Zoology*, London.

Bandura, A. (1971) 'Analysis of social modeling processes', in A. Bandura (ed.), *Psychological Modeling* (Chicago: Aldine Atherton).

Barlow, H. B. (1961) 'The coding of sensory messages,' in W. H. Thorpe and O. L. Zangwill (eds) *Current problems in Animal Behaviour* (Cambridge: Cambridge University Press).

Barnett, S. A. (1963) *A Study in Behaviour* (London: Methuen).
Barratt, C. L. (1969) 'Systematic desensitisation versus implosive therapy', *Journal of Abnormal Psychology*, 74, 587–92.
Basmajian, J. V. (1977) 'Learned control of single motor units', in G. E. Schartz and J. Beatty (eds), *Biofeedback: Theory and Research* (New York: Academic Press).
Bateman, A. J. (1948) 'Intra-sexual selection in drosophila', *Heredity*, 2 (3), 349–68.
Bateson, P. (1986) 'When to experiment on animals' *New Scientist*, 109, (1496) 30–2.
Batteau, D. W. and Markey, P. R. (1968) 'Man/dolphin communication', Final Report on contract N00123/67–1103, 15 Dec 1966, US Naval Ordnance Test Station, China Lake, California.
Birch, A. and Malim, T. (1988) *Development Psychology: from infancy to adulthood* (Basingstoke: Macmillan).
Blanchard, R., Fukunaga, K. and Blanchard, C. B. (1976) 'Environmental control of defensive reactions to a cat', *Bulletin of Psychonomic Society*, 8, 179–181.
Blanchard, E. B., Miller, S. T., Abel, G., Haynes, M. and Wicker, R. (1979) 'Evaluation of biofeedback in the treatment of borderline essential hypertension', *Journal of Applied Behaviour Analysis*, 12, 99–109.
Bornstein, M. H. (1988) 'Perceptual development across the life cycle', in M. H. Bornstein and M. E. Lamb (eds), *Perceptual, Cognitive and Linguistic Development* (Hove, E. Sussex: Lawrence Erlbaum Associates Ltd).
Bowlby, J. (1953, 2nd edn 1965) *Child care and the Growth of Love* (Harmondsworth, Penguin).
Bowlby, J. (1969) *Attachment and Loss, Vol. 1: Attachment*, (Harmondsworth: Penguin).
Brain, P. F., Benton, D. and Boulton, J. C. (1978) 'Comparison of agonistic behaviour in individually housed male mice and those co-habiting with females', *Aggressive Behaviour*, 4, 201–6.
Braine, M. D. S. (1963) 'The ontogeny of English phrase structure', *Language*, 39, 1–14.
Breland, K. and Breland, M. (1961) 'The misbehaviour of organisms', *American Psychologist*, 16, 681–4.
British Psychological Society (1985) 'A code of conduct for psychologists,' *Bulletin of the B.P.S.* vol. 38, pp. 41–3.
Brown, C. R. (1986) 'Cliff swallow colonies as information centres', *Science* (New York) 234, 83–5.
Brown, J. C. (1964) 'Observations of the elephant shrews (*Macroscelidae*) of equatorial Africa', *Proceedings of the Zoological Society of London*, 143(1), 103–19.
Brown, J. L. (1969) 'The buffer effect and productivity in tit populations', *American Nature*, 103, 347–54.
Brown, R. (1973) *The First Language: The Early Stages* (London: Allen & Unwin).
Brown, R. (1986) *Social Psychology*, 2nd edn (New York: Free Press).

Bustard, H. J. R. (1970) 'The role of behaviour in the natural regulation of numbers in the gekkonid lizard (*Gehyra variegata*)', *Ecology*, 51(4), 724–8.

Calhoun, J. (1962) 'Population density and social pathology', *Scientific American*, 206, 139–48.

Caraco, T., Martindale, S. and Pulliam, H. R. (1980) 'Flocking advantages and disadvantages', *Nature*, 285, 400–1.

Carl, E. A. (1971) 'Population control in arctic ground squirrels,' *Ecology* 52(3), 395–413.

Carr, W. J., Martrano, R. D. and Kramer, L (1970) 'Response of mice to odours associated with stress,' *Journal of Comparative and Physiological Psychology*, 71(2), 223–8.

Carrick, R., Csordas, S. E., Ingham, S. E. and Ingham, K. K. (1962) 'Studies on the Southern elephant seal (*Mirounga leonina*) – III and IV', *Wildlife Research*, Canberra, Australia.

Catchpole, C., Leisler, B. and Winkler, H. (1985) 'The evolution of polygyny in the great reed warbler (*Acrocephalus arundinaceus*): a possible case of deception', *Behavioural Ecological Sociobiology*, 16, 285–91.

Cavanagh, P. (1963) 'The autotutor and classroom instructions', *Occupational Psychology*, 37, 44–9.

Cheney, D. L. (1983) 'Extrafamiliar alliances among vervet monkeys', in R. A. Hinde (ed.), *Primate Social Relationships* (Oxford: Blackwell Scientific Publications).

Chomsky, N. (1972) *Language and Mind* (enlarged edition) (New York: Harcourt Brace Jovanovich).

Clark, H. H. and Malt, B. C. (1984) 'Psychological constraints on language: a commentary on Bresnan and Kaplan and on Givon', in W. Kintsch, J. R. Miller and P. G. Polson (eds), *Methods and Tactics in Cognitive Science* (Hillsdale, New Jersey: Erlbaum).

Clark, R. B. (1960) 'Habituation of the polychaete *Neries* to sudden stimuli. I General properties of the habituation process'. *Animal Behaviour*, 8, 82–91.

Clutton-Brock, T. H. and Albon, S. D. (1979) 'The roaring of red deer and evolution of honest advertisement', *Behaviour*, 69, 145–70.

Clutton-Brock, T. H. and Albon, S. D. (1989) *Red Deer in the Highlands* (Oxford: Professional Books).

Clutton-Brock, T. H., Guinness, F. E. and Albon, S. D. (1982) *Red deer: the behaviour and ecology of two sexes* (Chicago: Chicago University Press).

Coile, C. and Miller, N. E. (1984) 'How radical animal activists try to mislead humane people', *American Psychologist*, 39, 700–1.

Colvin, J. (1983) 'Description of siting and peer relationships among immature male rhesus monkeys', in R. A. Hinde (ed.), *Primate Social Relationships* (Oxford: Blackwell Scientific Publications).

Condon, W. D. and Sander, W. (1974) 'Neonate movement is synchronized with adult speech; interactional participation in language acquisition', *Science*, 183, 99–101.

Coon, D. (1983) *Introduction to Psychology* 3rd edn (St Paul, Minnesota: West Publishing Co).

Crook, J. H. (1964) 'The evolution of social organisation and visual communication in the weaver birds (*Ploceinae*), *Behaviour*, Supplement 10, pp. 178 ff.

Crook, J. H. (1965) 'The adaptive significance of avian social organisations', *Symposium of the Zoological Society of London*, 14, 181–218.

Crook, J. H. (1970) 'Social organisation and the environment: aspects of contemporary social ethology', *Animal Behaviour*, 18, 197–209.

Curzon, L. (1980) *Teaching in Further Education* (London: Cassell).

Cuthill I. (1991) 'Field experiments in animal behaviour: Methods and ethics', *Animal Behaviour* 42 (6), 1006–14.

Dagan, D. and Volman, S. (1982) Sensory basis for wind direction in first instar cockroaches, *Periplaneta Americana and Journal of Comparative Physiology* 147: 471–8.

Dane, B., Walcott, C. and Drury, W. H. (1959) 'The form and duration of the display actions of the ÒgoldeneyeÓ', *Behaviour*, 14, 265–81.

Darling, F. F. (1935) *A Herd of Red Deer* (London: Oxford University Press).

Darling F. F. (1938) *Bird Flocks and the Breeding Cycle: A Contribution to Avian Sociality* (Cambridge: Cambridge University Press).

Darwin, C. (1859) *The Origin of Species* (London: Collins).

Darwin, C. (1872) *Expressions of Emotion in Man and Animals* (London: John Murray).

Davies, N. B. (1989) 'Sexual conflict and the polygyny threshold', *Animal Behaviour*, 38, 226–34.

Davies, N. B. and Brooke, M. de L. (1989) 'An experimental study of co-evolution between the cuckoo and its hosts', *Journal of Animal Ecology*, 58, 225–36.

Dawkins, R. (1976) *The Selfish Gene* (Oxford: Oxford University Press).

Dawkins, M. (1990) 'From an animal's point of view; motivation, fitness and animal welfare', *Behaviour and Brain Sciences*, 13 (1), 1–61.

Deag, J. M. (1977) 'Aggression and submission in monkey societies', *Animal Behaviour*, 25, 465–77.

Deutsch, J. A. (1960) *The Structural Basis of Behaviour* (London: Cambridge University Press. Copyright 1960 by the University of Chicago. Published 1960, composed and printed by the University of Chicago Press, Chicago, Illinois.

Diament, C. and Wilson, G. T. (1975) 'An experimental investigation of the effects of covert sensitisation in an analogue eating situation', *Behaviour Therapy*, 6, 499–509.

Dunnett, S., Lane, D. and Winn, P. (1985) 'Ibotenic acid lesions of the lateral hypothalamus: comparison with 6-hydroxydopamine-induced sensorimotor deficits', *Neuroscience*, 14, 509–18.

Elgar, M. A. (1986) 'House sparrows establish foraging flocks by giving chirrup calls if the resources are divisible', *Animal Behaviour* 34, 169–174.

Elgar, M. (1989) 'Predator vigilance and group size among mammals and birds: a critical review of the evidence', *Biological Review*, 64 1–34.

Emlen, S. and Oring L. W. (1977) 'Ecology, sexual selection and the evolution of mating systems', *Science* (New York), 197, 215–23.

Erber, J. (1981) 'Neural correlates of learning in the honey bee', *Trends in Neurosciences*, 4, 270–3.

Esch, H., Esch, I. and Kerr, W. E. (1965) 'Sound: an element common to communication of stingless bees and dances of honey bees', *Science* (New York), 149, 320–1.

Estes, W. K. (1970) *Learning Theory and Mental Development* (New York: Academic Press).

Estes, W. K. (1944) 'An experimental study of punishment' *Psychology Monograph* 57, No. 263.

Fonagy, P. and Higgitt, A. (1984) *Personality Theory and Clinical Practice* (London: Methuen).

Fouts, R. S. (1972) 'The use of guidance in teaching sign language to a chipanzee', *Journal of Comparative Physiological Psychology*, 80, 515–22.

Freud, A. and Dann, S. (1951) 'An experiment in group upbringing' in *Psychoanalytic Study of the Child*, Vol. VI.

Fraser, A. F. and Broom, D. M. (1990) *Farm Animal Behaviour and Welfare* (London: Bailliere Tindall; and New York: Saunders).

Frisch, K. von (1967) *The Dance Language and Orientation of Bees* (Cambridge, Mass.: The Belknap Press of Harvard University).

Gardner, R. A. and Gardner, B. T. (1969) 'Teaching sign language to a chimpanzee', *Science*, 165, 664–2.

Geddes, P. (1885) 'An analysis of the principles of economics (part I)', Paper read before the Royal Society of Edinburgh, July 1885.

Geist, V. (1971) *Mountain Sheep: A Study in Behaviour and Evolution* (Chicago: University of Chicago Press).

Gellerman, L. W. (1933) 'Form discrimination in chimpanzees and two-year-old children: I Form (triangularity) per se', *Journal of Genetic Psychology*, 42, 3–27.

Gibson, R. M. and Bradbury, J. W. (1985) 'Sexual selection in lekking sage grouse: phenotypic correlates of male mating success', *Behavioural Ecological Sociobiology*, 18, 117–23.

Gill, F. B. and Wolf, L. L. (1975) 'Economics of feeding territoriality in the golden winged sunbird', *Ecology*, 56, 333–45.

Goodall, J. van Lawick (1968) 'The behaviour of free living chimpanzees in the Gombe Stream Reserve', *Animal Behaviour Monograph* 1, 161–311.

Goodall, J. van Lawick (1974) *In the Shadow of Man* (London: Fontana).

Göttmark F. and Andersson, M. (1984) 'Colonial breeding reduces nest predation in the common gull', *Animal Behaviour*, 32, 323–33.

Gould, J. L. (1976) 'The dance language controversy', *Quarterly Review of Biology*, 51, 211–44.

Gould, S. J. (1981) *The Mismeasure of Man* (New York: Norton).

Gould J. L., Dyer, F. C. and Towne, W. F. (1985) 'Recent progress in understanding the honey bee dance language', *Fortschritte der Zoologie*, 31, 141–61.

Gouzoules, S. and Gouzoules, H. (1987) 'Kinship', in B. B. Smuts, D. L. Cheney, R. M. Seyfarth, R. W. Wrangham and T. T. Struhsacker (eds), *Primate Studies* (Chicago: University of Chicago Press).

Grafen, A. (1990) 'Biological signals as handicaps', *Journal of Theoretical Biology*, 144, 517–25.

Gramza, A. F. (1967) 'Responses of brooding night hawks to a disturbance stimulus', *Auk* 84(1), 72–86.

Gray, J. A. (1987) 'The Ethnics and politics of animal experimentation' in H. Beloff and A. M. Colman (eds) *Psychological Survey No. 6* (Leicester: The British Psychological Society).

Griffin, D. R. (1958) *Listening in the Dark* (New Haven, Conn.: Yale University Press).

Griffin, D. R. (1984) *Animal Thinking* (Cambridge, Mass.: Harvard University Press).

Guiton, P. (1959) 'Socialisation and imprinting in Brown Leghorn chicks, *Animal Behaviour*, 16, 261–94.

Haartman, L. von (1969) 'Nest site and the evolution of polygyny in European passerine birds', *Ornis Fennica*, 46(1) 1–12.

Hall, K. R. L. (1960) 'Social vigilance behaviour of the chacma baboon (*Papio ursinus*)', *Behaviour*, 16, 261–94.

Hamilton, W. D. (1971a) 'Selfish and spiteful behaviour in an evolutionary model', *Nature (London)*, 228(5277), 1218–20.

Hamilton, W. D. (1971b) 'Geometry for the selfish herd', *Journal of Theoretical Biology*, 31, 295–311.

Hamilton, W. D. and Zuk, M. (1984) 'Heritable true fitness and bright birds: a role for parasites?', *Science (New York)*, 218, 384–7.

Hardie, J. Keir (1907) *From Serfdom to Socialism* (London: Geo. Allen).

Harlow, H. F. (1949) 'The formation of learning sets', *Psychological Review*, 56, 51–65.

Harlow, H. F., Harlow, M. K. and Meyer, D. R. (1950) Learning motivated by a manipulation drive. Journal of *Experimental Psychology*, 40, 228–234.

Harlow, A. F. and Harlow, M. K. (1965) 'The affectional systems,' in Schrier, A. M., Harlow, A. F. and Stollnitz, F. (eds) *Behaviour of Non-Human Primates*, Vol 2 (New York: Academic Press).

Hayes, C. (1951) *The Ape in Our House* (New York: Harper & Rowe).

Hayes, K. J. and Hayes, C. (1952) 'Imitation in a home raised chimpanzee', *Journal of Comparative and Physiological Psychology*, 45, 450–9.

Hayes, N. (1986) 'The magic of sociobiology', *Psychology Teaching*, part 2, 2–16.

Hebb, D. O. (1958) *A Textbook of Psychology* (P. Saunders).

Heiligenberg, W. and Kramer, U. (1972) 'Aggressiveness as a function of external stimulation' *Journal of Comparative Physiology*, 77, 332–40.

Herman, L., Richards, D. G. and Wolz, J. P. (1984) 'Comprehension of sentences by bottle-nosed dolphins', *Cognition*, 16, 129–219.

Hess, E. H. (1972) 'Imprinting in a natural laboratory' in *Psychology in Progress: Readings from Scientific American* (San Francisco: W. H. Freeman).

Hinde, R. A. and Rowell, T. E. (1962) 'Communication by postures and facial expressions in the rhesus monkey (*Macaca mulatta*)', *Proceeding of the Zoological Society of London*, 138, 1–21.

Hinde, R. A. (1987) *Individuals, Relationships and Culture: Links between Ethology and the Social Sciences* (Cambridge: Cambridge University Press).

Hockett, C. F. (1959) 'Animal languages and human language', *Human Biology*, 31, 32–9.

Hockett, C. F. (1960) 'The origin of speech', *Scientific American*, 203, 8–96.

Holmes, W. G. and Sherman, P. W. (1982) 'The ontogeny of kin recognition in two species of ground squirrels', *American Zoologist*, 22, 491–597.

Hoogland, W. G. and Sherman, P. W. (1976) 'Advantages and disadvantages of bank swallow coloniality', *Ecological Monograph*, 46, 33–58.

Hooker, T. and Hooker, Barbara I. (1969) 'Duetting' in R. A Hinde (ed.), *Bird Vocalizations: Their Relations to Current Problems in Biology and Psychology: Essays presented to W. H. Thorpe* (Cambridge: Cambridge University Press).

Horn, G. (1985) *Memory, Imprinting and the Brain* (Oxford: Clarendon Press).

Horn, G. (1990) 'Neural bases of recognition memory investigated through an analysis of imprinting', *Phil. Trans. Royal Society London B*, 329, 133–42.

Hull, C. (1943) *Principles of Behaviour* (New York: Appleton Century Crofts).

Humphrey, N. K. (1976) 'The social function of intellect', in P. P. G. Bateson and R. A. Hinde (eds), *Growing Points in Ethology* (Cambridge: Cambridge University Press).

Huxley, J. S. (1914) *The courtship habits of the great crested grebe, Podiceps cristatus*. Proceedings of the Zoological Society, London 1914 (2): 491–562.

Janowitz, H. D. and Grossman, M. I. (1949) 'Some factors influencing the food intake of normal dogs and dogs with oesophagotomy and gastric fistulas', *American Journal of Physiology*, 159, 143–8.

Janowitz, H. D. and Grossman M. I. (1949) 'Some factors affecting the food intake of normal dogs and dogs with esophagostomy and gastric fistula', *American Journal of Physiology*, 56, 137–59.Jarman, P. J. (1974) 'The social organisation of the antelope in relation to ecology', *Behaviour*, 48, 215–55.

Jerison, H. J. (1985) 'Animal intelligence and encephalization', *Phil. Trans. Royal Society London B*, 308, 21–35.

Jolly, A. (1966) *Lemur Behaviour* (Chicago: Chicago University Press).

Jones, S. (1993) *The Language of the Genes* (London: HarperCollins Flamingo).

Kacelnik, A. (1984) 'Central place foraging in starlings, Sturnus Vulgaris', *Journal of Animal Ecology*, 53, 283–299.

Kaye, K. and Brazelton, T. B. (1971) 'Mother and infant interaction in the organisation of sucking', Paper delivered to the Society for Research into Child Development, Minneapolis, USA.

Kazdin, A. E. (1977) *Advances in Clinical Child Psychology*, Vol. 1 (eds) B. B. Lahey and A. E. Kazdin (New York: Plenum Press).

Kellogg, W. N. and Kellogg, L. A. (1933) *The Ape and the Child* (New York: McGraw Hill).

Koestler, A. (1970) *The Ghost in the Machine* (London: Pan Books).

Köhler, W. (1927) *The Mentality of Apes*, 2nd edn (London: Kegan Paul).

Konishi M. (1965) 'The role of auditory feedback on the control of vocalisation in the white-crowned sparrow', *Zeitschrift für Tierpsychologie*, 22, 770–83.

Krebs, J. R. and Davies, N. D. (1987) *An Introduction to Behavioural Ecology* (2nd edn) (Blackwell: Oxford).

Kruijt, J. P. (1964) 'Ontogeny of social behaviour in Burmese red jungle fowl *(Gallus gallus spadiceus)*', *Behaviour*, 12, 1–201.

Kuhn, T. S. (1962) *The Structure of Scientific Revolutions* (Chicago, Illinois: University of Chicago Press).

Kruuk, H. (1972) *The Spotted Hyena* (Chicago: Chicago University Press).

Kummer, H. (1968) 'Two variations in the social organisation of baboons', in P. Jay, *Primates: Studies in Adaptation and Variability* (New York and London: Holt Rinehart & Winston).

Lazarus, J. (1979) 'The early warning function of flocking in birds: an experimental study with captive quelea', *Animal Behaviour*, 27, 855–65.

Lea, S. E.G. (1984) *Instinct, Environment and Behaviour* (London: Methuen).

Le Boeuf, B. J. (1974) 'Male–male competition and reproductive success in elephant seals', *American Zoologist*, 14, 163–76.

Leyhausen, P. (1956) 'Verhaltenstudien an Katzen', *Zeitschrift für Tierpsychologie*, Supplement 2, vi, 120pp.

Lorenz, K. Z. (1937) 'The companion in the birds' world', *Auk*, 54, 24–73.

Lorenz, K. (1950) 'The comparative method in studying innate behaviours', *Symposium of the Experimental Biological Society*, 221–68.

Lorenz, K. Z. (1952) *King Solomon's Ring* (London: Methuen).

Lorenz, K. Z. (1958) 'The evolution of behaviour', *Scientific American*, 199 (6), 67–78.

Lorenz, K. Z. (1966) *On Aggression* (London: Methuen).

Lorenz, K. and Tinbergen, N. (1970) 'Taxis and behaviour patterns in egg-rolling by the greylag goose', in: Lorenz, K., *Studies in human and animal behaviour* (London: Methuen).

Lovaas, O. I., Keogel, R., Simmons, J. and Long, J. (1973) 'Some generalisation and follow-up measures on autistic children in behaviour therapy', *Journal of Applied Behaviour Analysis*, 6, 131–66.

Lumsden, C. J and Wilson, E. O. (1983) *Promethean Fire* (Cambridge, Mass.: Harvard University Press).

Macdonald, D. W. (1986) 'A meerkat volunteers for guard duty so its comrades can live in peace', *Smithsonian*, April 1985, 55–84.

MacFarlane, A. (1975) 'Olfaction in the development of social preferences in the human neonate', in Porter R. and O'Connor M. (eds), *Parent–Infant Interaction*, (Amsterdam: Elsevier).

Mackintosh, N. J. (1983) 'General principles of learning', in T. R. Halliday and P. J. B. Slater (eds), *Animal Behaviour, Vol. 3 Genes, Development and Learning* (Oxford: Blackwell Scientific) pp. 149–77.

Mackintosh, N. J., Wilson, B. and Boakes, R. A. (1985) 'Differences in mechanisms of intelligence among vertebrates', *Phil. Trans. Roy. Soc. of Lond. B* 308, 53–65.

Macphail, E. (1985) 'Vertebrate intelligence: the null hypothesis', *Philosophical Transcript. Royal Society of London B*, 308, 37–51.

Macphail, E. M. (1987) 'The comparative psychology of intelligence', *Behavioural Brain Science*, 10, 645–95.

Magnus (1958) 'Experimentelle Untersuchungen zur Bionomie und Ethologie des Kaisermantels (*Argynnis paphia L.*) I. Über optische Auslöser Anflieghreaktionen und ihrer Bedeutung für das Sichfinden der Geschlechter', *Zeitschrift fær Tierpsychologie*, 15, 307–426.

Maier, N. R. F. and Schneirla, T. C. (1935) *Principles of Animal Psychology* (New York: McGraw-Hill).

Malim, T. Birch, A. and Wadeley A. (1992) *Perspectives in Psychology* (Basingstoke: Macmillan).

Malim, A. (1994) *Cognitive Psychology* (Basingstoke: Macmillan).

Manning, M. and Dawkins, M. S. (1992) *Animal Behaviour*, 4th edn (Cambridge University Press).

Marks, I. M. (1981) 'Review of behavioral psychotherapy: I Obsessive–compulsive disorders', *American Journal of Psychiatry*, 138, 584–92.

Marler, P. and Tamura, M. (1964) 'Culturally transmitted patterns of vocal behaviour in sparrow', *Science (NY)*, 146, 1483–6.

Martin, G. M. and Lett, B. T. (1985) 'Formation of associations of colored and flavoured food with induced sickness in five main species', *Behavioural and Neural Biology*, 43, 223–37.

Martinez, D. R. and Klinghammer (1970) 'The behaviour of the whale (*Orcinus orca*): a review of the literature', *Zeitschrif für Tierpsychologie*, 27(7), 828–39.

Maschwitz, U. (1964) 'Gefahrenalarmstoffe und Gefahrenalarmierung bei sozialen Hymenopteren, *Zeitschrift für Vergleichende Psychologie* 47(6) 596–655.

Maschwitz, U. (1966) 'Alarm substances and alarm behaviour in social insects', *Vitamins and Hormones*, 24, 267–90.

Maslow, A. (1970) *Motivation and Personality* (New York: Harper & Row).

Masserman, J. H. (1950) 'Experimental neuroses', *Scientific American*, 182(3), 38–43.

Maynard-Smith, J. (1976) 'Evolution and the theory of games', *American Scientist* 64, 41–5.

Maynard-Smith, J. (1982) *Evolution and Theory of Games* (Cambridge: Cambridge University Press).

Maynard-Smith, J. and Riechert, S. E. (1984) 'A conflicting-tendency model of spider agonistic behaviour: hybrid-pure population line comparison', *Animal Behaviour*, 32, 564.

McFarland, D. J. (1971) *Feedback mechanisms in animal behaviour* (New York: Academic Press).

McGaugh, J. L. (1989) 'Involvement of hormonal and neuromodulatory systems in the regulation of memory storage', *Annual Review Neuroscience*, 12, 255–87.

McGlynn, F. D., Mealiea, W. L. and Landau, D. L. (1981) 'The current status of systematic desensitization', *Clinical Psychology Review*, 1, 149–79.

McGrew, W. C., Tutin, C. E. G. and Baldwin, P. J. (1979) 'Chimpanzees, tools and termites: Cross-cultural comparisons of Senegal, Tanzania and Rio Muni' *Man* 14, 185–215.

McNeill, D. (1970) *The Acquisition of Language* (New York: Harper & Row).

Mehler, J., Bertoncini, J., Barnière, M. and Jassik-Gerschenfeld, D. (1978) 'Infant recognition of mother's voice', *Perception* 7, 491–7.

Melzack, R., Penick, E. and Beckett, A. (1959) 'The problem of innate fear of hawk shape, an experimental study with mallard ducks', *Journal of Comparative Physiological Psychology*, 52, 694–8.

Michelsen, A. (1989) 'Ein mechanisches Modell der tanzenden Honigbiene', *Biologie in unserer Zeit*, 19 (4), 121–6.

Michelsen, A., Andersen, B. B., Kirchner, W. H. and Lindauer, M. (1989) 'Honey bees can be recruited by a mechanical model of a dancing bee', *Naturwissenschaften*, 76, 277–80.

Milinski, M. and Heller, R. (1978) 'Influence of a predator on the optimal foraging behaviour of sticklebacks (*Gasterosteus aculeatus*)', *Nature* (London), 275, 642–4.

Miller, N. E. Sampliner, R. I. and Woodrow, P. (1957) 'Thirst-reducing effects of water by stomach fistula vs water by mouth, measured by both a consummatory and an instrumental response, *Journal of Comparative Physiological Psychology*, 50, 1–5.

Miller, N. and DiCara, L. (1967) 'Instrumental learning of heart rate changes in curarised rats, shaping and specificity to discriminating stimulus', *Journal of Comparative and Physiological Psychology*, 63, 12–19.

Mishkin, M. and Appenzeller, T. (1987) 'The anatomy of memory', *Scientific American* 256(6), 62–71.

Mitchell, G. D. (1964) 'Paternalistic behaviour in primates,' *Psychological Bulletin*, 71, 399–417.

Moore, B. R. (1973) 'The role of directed Pavlovian reactions in simple instrumental learning in the pigeon', in R. A. Hinde and J. Stevenson-Hinde (eds), *Constraints on Learning*, (London: Academic Press) pp. 159–88.

Morgan, L. (1894) *An Introduction to Comparative Psychology* (London: Scott).

Morris, D. (1959) 'The comparative ethology of grassfinches and mannikins', *Proceedings of the Zoological Society of London*, 131, 389–439.

Morris, D. (1977) *Manwatching* (St. Albans: Panther).

Moruzzi, G. and Magoun, H. W. (1949) 'Brain stem reticular formation and activation of the EEG', *Electroencephalographic Clinical Neurophysiology*, 1, 455–473.

Mowrer, O. H. (1950) *Learning Theory and Personality Dynamics* (New York: Roland Press).

Munn, R. L. (1950) *Handbook of Psychological Research on the Rat* (Boston, Mass.: Houghton Mifflin).

Namikas, J. and Wehmer, F. (1978) 'Gender composition of the litter affects the behaviour of male mice', *Behavioural Biology*, 23, 219–24.

Nelson, B. (1980) *Sea Birds: their Biology and Ecology* (London: Hamlyn).

Noble, G. K. ((1936) 'Courtship and sexual selection of the flicker (*Colaptes auratus luteus*)', *Auk*, 53, 269–82.

Numan, M. (1974) 'Medial preoptic area and maternal behaviour in the female rat', *Journal of Comparative and Physiological Psychology*, 87, 746–59.

Olds, J. and Milner, P. (1954) 'Positive reinforcement produced by electrical stimulation of septal area and other regions of rat brain', *Journal of Comparative Physiological Psychology*, 47, 419–27.

Olton, D. S. (1979) 'Mazes, maps and memory', *American Psychologist*, 34, 583–96.

Orians, G. (1969) 'On the evolution of mating systems in birds and mammals', *American Nature*, 103, 589–603.

Packer, C. (1986) 'The ecology of sociality in felids', in Rubenstein D. I. and Wrangham R. W. (eds) *Ecological Aspects of Social Evolution*, (Princeton, New Jersey: Princeton University Press).

Parkes, C. M. (1972) *Bereavement: Studies of Grief in Adult life*, (Harmondsworth: Penguin).

Patterson, F. G. (1978) 'The gestures of a gorilla: language acquisition in another pongid', *Brain and Language*, 5, 72–97.

Patterson, F. G. (1979) 'Conversation with a Gorilla', *National Geographic*, 154 (4), 438–65.

Paul, G. L. and Lentz, R. (1977) *Psychosocial Treatment of Chronic Mental Patients: Milieu versus Social Learning Programs* (Cambridge, Mass: Harvard University Press).

Pavlov, I. (1927) (trans. G.V. Anrep) *Conditioned Reflexes* (London: Oxford University Press).

Payne, R. S. and McVay, S. (1971) 'Songs of humpback whales', *Science*, 173, 585–97.

Peck, J. and Blass, E. (1975) 'Localisation of thirst and antidiuretic osmoreceptors by intracranial injections in rats', *American Journal of Physiology*, 5, 1501–9.

Peek, F. W. (1971) 'Seasonal change in the breeding behaviour of the male red winged blackbird (agelaus phoeniceus)', *Wilson Bulletin*, 83(4), 393–5.

Pepperberg, I. M. (1983) 'Cognition in the African grey parrot: preliminary evidence for auditory/vocal comprehension of the class concept', *Animal Learning Behaviour*, 11, 179–85.

Pepperberg, I. M. (1987) 'Interspecies communication: a tool for assessing capabilities in the African grey parrot (*Psittacus erithracus*)', in G. Greenberg and E. Tobach (eds), *Language Cognition and Consciousness: Integrative Levels* (Hillsdale N.J.: Erlbaum).

Pepperberg, I. M. (1990) 'Some cognitive capacities of an African grey parrot (*Psittacus erithracus*)', *Advances in the Study of Behaviour*, 19, 357–409.

Piaget, J. (1952) *Origins of Intelligence in Children* (trans M. Cook) (New York: Int. University Press).

Plummer, S., Baer, D. and LeBlanc, J. (1977) 'Functional consideration in the use of time-out and an effective alternative', *Journal of Applied Behaviour Analysis*, 10, 689–706.

Polis, G. E. (1981) 'The evolution and dynamics of intra-specific predation', in Johnson, R. F., Frank, P. W. and Michener, C. D. (eds) *Annual*

Review of Systematics, Vol 2 (Palo Alto, California: Annual Reviews)

Powell, G. V. N. (1974) 'Experimental analysis of the social value of flocking by starlings (asturnus vulgaris) in relation to predation and foraging', *Animal Behaviour*, 22, 501–5.

Premack, A. J. and Premack, D. (1972) 'Teaching language to an ape', *Scientific American*, 227, 92–9.

Premack, D. and Woodruff, G. (1978) 'Does the chimpanzee have a theory of mind?', *Behavioural Brain Science*, 1, 515–26.

Pressey, S. L. (1926) 'A simple apparatus which gives tests and scores – and teaches' *School and Society*, 23, 373–76.

Pulliam, H. R. (1976) 'The principle of optimal behaviour and the theory of communities', in P. H. Klopfer and P. P. G. Bateson (eds), *Perspectives in Ethology* (New York: Plenum Press) pp. 311–32.

Rachman, S. and Wilson, G. (1980) *The Effects of Psychological Therapy* (Oxford: Pergamon).

Rand, A. S. and Rand, W. M. (1978) 'Display and dispute settlement in nesting iguanas', in M. Greenberg and P. O. MacLean (eds), *Behaviour and Neurology of Lizards* (Rockville, Md.: National Inst. of Mental Health).

Rescorla, R. A. (1988) 'Pavlovian conditioning: it's not what you think it is', *American Psychologist*, 43, 151–60.

Riechart, S. (1984) 'Games spiders play III. Cues underlying context associated changes in agonistic behaviour', *Animal Behaviour*, 32, 1–15.

Riechart, S. and Maynard-Smith, J. (1989) 'Genetic analysis of two behavioural traits linked to individual fitness in the desert spider (agelopsis aperta)', *Animal Behaviour*, 37, 624–37.

Rohwer, S. and Rohwer, F. C. (1978) 'Status signalling in Harris sparrows: experimental deceptions achieved', *Animal Behaviour* 26, 1012–22.

Roper, T. J. (1984) 'Response of thirsty rats to absence of water: frustration, disinhibition and compensation', *Animal Behaviour*, 32, 1225–35.

Rose, S., Kamin, L. J. and Lewontin, R. C. (1990) *Our Genes: Biology Ideology and Human Nature* (Harmondsworth: Penguin).

Rowell, C. H. F. (1961) 'Displacement grooming in the chaffinch', *Animal Behaviour*, 9, 38–63.

Rowell, T. E., Hinde, R. A. and Spencer-Booth, Y. (1964) '"Aunt"; Infant interaction in captive rhesus monkeys', *Animal Behaviour*, 12, 219–26.

Rowell, T. (1974) 'The concept of social dominance', *Behavioural Biology*, 2, 131–54.

Rowland, W. J. (1989) 'Mate choice and the supernormality effect in female sticklebacks (*Gasterosteus aculeatus*)', *Behavioural Ecological Sociobiology* 24, 433–8.

Rumbaugh, D. M. (1976) *Language Learning by a Chimpaanzee: The Lana Project* (New York: Academic Press).

Rutter, M. (1972) *Maternal Deprivation Re-assessed* (Harmondsworth: Penguin).

Ryan, C. M. E. (1982) 'Mechanisms of individual recognition in birds', unpublished M.Phil. dissertation, University of Exeter.

Saayman, G. S. (1971) 'Aggressive behaviour in free-ranging chacma baboons (Papio ursinus)', *Journal of Behavioural Science*, 1, 77–83.

Sachs, B. and Meisel, R. (1988) 'The physiology of male sexual behaviour', in E. Knobil and J. Neill (eds), *The Physiology of Reproduction* (New York: Raven Press).

Savage-Rumbaugh, E. S., Pate, J. L., Lawson, J., Smith, T. and Rosenbaum, S. (1983) 'Can a chimpanzee make a statement?' *Journal of Experimental Psychology: General*, 112, 457–92.

Schelderup-Ebbe, T. (1935) 'Social behaviour of birds', in C. Murchison (ed.) *Handbook of Social Psychology* (Worcester, Mass.: Clark University Press).

Schiller, P. H. (1957) 'Manipulative patterns in the chimpanzee', in Schiller, P. H. (ed.) *Instinctive Behaviour* (London: Methuen).

Schleidt, W. M., Schleidt, M. and Magg, M. (1960) 'Störung der Mutter-Kind-Beziehung bei Truthühnein durch Gehöverlust', *Behaviour*, 16, 254–60.

Schleidt, W. M. (1961) 'Reaktionenen von Truthühnen auf fliegende Raubvögel und Versuch der Analyse ihrer AAM's', *Zeitschvift für Tierpsychologie*, 18, 534–602.

Schmid-Hempel, P., Kacelnik, A. and Houston, A. I. (1985) 'Honeybees maximise efficiency by not filling their crop', *Behaviour Ecology and Sociobiology*, 17, 61–66.

Schneirla, T. C. (1966) 'Behavioural development and comparative psychology', *Quarterly Review of Biology*, 41, 283–302.

Schoener, T. W. and Schoener, Amy (1971) 'Structural habitats of West Indian anolis lizards, I Lowland Jamaica', *Breviora*, pp. 368ff.

Seeley, T. (1985) *Honeybee ecology* (New Jersey: Princetown University Press).

Selander, R. K. (1972) 'Sexual selection and dimorphism in birds', in B. Campbell (ed.) *Sexual Selection and the Descent of Man 1871–1971* (Chicago: Aldine Publ. Co.).

Sevenster, P. (1961) 'Causal analysis of a displacement activity (fanning) in *Gasterosteus aculeatus* L.', *Behavioural Supplement*, 2, (9), 1–170.

Shaikh, M. and Siegel, A. (1989) 'Naloxone-induced modulation of feline aggression elicited from midbrain periaqueductal gray', *Pharmacology, Biochemistry and Behaviour*, 31, 791–6.

Shapiro, D. and Surwit, R. S. (1979) 'Biofeedback', in O. F. Pommerleau and J. P. Brady (eds), *Behavioural Medicine: Theory and Practice* (Baltimore: Williams & Wilkins).

Skinner, B. F. (1938) *The Behaviour of Organisms* (New York: Appleton-Century-Crofts).

Skinner, B. F. (1954) 'The science of learning and the art of teaching' *Harvard Educational Review*. 24, 86–97.

Spencer, H. (1851) *Social Statics* (London: Williams & Norgale).

Spencer, H. (1884) *Man versus the State: Essays Reprinted, from Contemporary Review Feb–Jul 1884* (Harmondsworth: Penguin).

Sterman, H. B. (1973) 'Neorphysiological and clinical studies of sensorimotor EEG feedback training: some effects on epilepsy', *Seminars in Psychiatry*, 5, 507–25.

Svare, B. and Gandelman, R. (1976) 'Postpartum aggression in mice: the influence of suckling stimulation', *Hormones and Behaviour*, 7, 407–16.

Taylor, A., Sluckin, W., Davies, D. R., Reason, J. T., Thomson, R. and Colman, A. M. (1982) *Introducing Psychology* (Harmondsworth: Penguin).

Terrace, H. S. (1979) 'How Nim Chimpsky changed my mind', *Psychology Today*, 13, 65–76.

Terrace, H. S., Pettito, L. A., Sanders, D. J. and Bever, T. G. (1979) 'On the grammatical capacities in apes', in *Children's Language Vol. II* (New York: Gardner Press).

Thorndike, E. L. (1913) *Educational Psychology* (New York: Columbia University Press).

Thorpe, W. H. (1963) *Learning and Instinct in Animals*, 2nd edn (London: Methuen).

Tinbergen, N. and Perdeck, E. C. (1950) 'On the stimulus situation releasing the begging response in the newly hatched herring-gull chick', *Behaviour*, 3, 1–39.

Tinbergen, N. (1951) *The Study of Instinct* (Oxford: Oxford University Press).

Tinbergen, N. (1959) 'Comparative studies of the behaviour of gulls (*Laridae*): a progress report', *Behavior*, 15, 1–70.

Tinbergen, N. (1967) 'Adaptive features of the black-headed gull (larus ridibundus)', *Proceedings of 14th International Ornithological Congress, Oxford 1966*, pp. 43–59.

Toates, F. (1986) *Motivational systems* (Cambridge: Cambridge University Press).

Todt, D. (1975) 'Social learning of vocal patterns and models of their applications in grey parrots', *Zeitschrift für Tierpsychologie*, 39, 178–88.

Tolman, E. C. (1932) *Purposive Behaviour in Animals and Men* (New York: The Century Co.).

Trevarthen, C. (1974) 'Conversations with a one-month-old', *New Scientist*, 62, 230–5.

Trevarthen, C. (1975) 'Early attempts at speech' in Lewin, R. (ed.) *Child Alive* (London: Temple Smith).

Trevarthen, C. (1977) 'Descriptive analyses of infant communicative behaviour', in Schaffer, H. R. (ed.) *Studies in Mother-Infant Interaction* (London: Academic Press).

Trivers, R. L. (1972) 'Parental investment and sexual selection', in B. Campbell (ed.), *Sexual Selection and the Descent of Man 1871–1971* (Chicago: Aldine Publ. Co.).

Trivers, R. L. (1971) 'The evolution of reciprocal altruism', *Quarterly Review of Biology*, 46(4), 35–57.

Trivers, R. L. (1974) 'Parent Offspring Conflict,' *American Zoologist* 14, 249–69.

Verner, J. (1965) 'Breeding biology of the long-billed marsh wren', *Condor*, 67 (1), 6–30.

Verner, J. and Wilson, M. F. (1966) 'The influence of habitats on mating systems of N. American passerine birds', *Ecology*, 47, 143–7.

Vestergaard, K. (1980) 'The regulation of dust bathing and other patterns in the laying hen: a Lorenzian approach', in R. Moss (ed.), *The Laying*

Hen and its Environment (The Hague: Martinus Nijhoff).

Vines, G. (1981) 'Wolves in dog's clothing', *New Scientist*, 91, 648–52.

Voci, V. and Carlson, N. R. (1973) 'Enhancement of maternal behaviour and nest behaviour following systemic and diencephalic administration of prolactin and progesterone in the mouse', *Journal of Comparative and Physiological Psychology*, 83, 388–93.

Vom Saal, F. S. and Bronson, F. (1980) 'Sexual characteristics of adult females correlates with their blood testosterone levels during development in mice', *Science* (NY), 208, 597–9.

Vowles, D. M. (1965) 'Maze learning and visual discrimination in the wood ant (*Formica rufa*)', *British Journal of Psychology*, 56, 15–31.

Vygotsky, L. S. (1962) *Thought and Language* (Cambridge, Mass.: MIT Press).

Waal, F. van der (1989) *Chimpanzee Politics* (Baltimore, Md.: Johns Hopkins University Press).

Walker, S. (1984) *Learning Theory and Behaviour Modification* (London: Methuen).

Wallace, A. R. (1981) *Natural Selection and Tropical Nature* (London: Macmillan).

Warren, J. M. (1965) 'Primate learning in comparative perspective', in A. M. Schrier, H. F. Harlow and F. Stollnitz (eds), *Behaviour of Nonhuman Primates*, Vol. 1 (New York: Academic Press) pp. 249–81.

Watson, J. (1913) 'Psychology as the behaviourist views it', *Psychological Review*, 20, 158–77.

Wells, M. J. (1962) *Brain and Behaviour in Cephalopods* (London: Heinemann Educational).

Wells, P. H. and Wenner, A. M. (1973) 'Do honey bees have a language', *Nature* (London), 4, 28–38.

Werner, E. E., Gilliam, J. F., Hall, D. J. and Mittlebach, G. E. (1983) 'An experimental test of the effects of predation risk on habitat use in fish', *Ecology*, 64, 1540–8.

Whitehead, L. (1979) 'Sex differences in children's responses to family stress: a re-evaluation', *J. Psychology & Psychiatry*, 20, 247–54.

Wilkinson, P. F. and Shank, C. C. (1977) 'Rutting-fight mortality among musk oxen on Banks Island, Northwest territories, Canada', *Animal Behaviour*, 24, 756–8.

Wilkinson, G. S. (1984) 'Reciprocal food sharing in the vampire bat', *Nature (London)*, 308, 181–4.

Williams, L., Martin, G., McDonald, S., Hardy, L. and Lambert, L. (snr) (1975) 'Effects of backscratch contingency of reinforcement for table serving on social interaction with severely retarded girls', *Behaviour Therapy*, 6, 220–9.

Wilson, E. O. (1965) 'Chemical communication in social imsects', *Science (NY)* 149, 1064–7.

Wilson, E. O. (1971) *The Insect Societies* (Cambridge, Mass.: Belknap Press of Harvard University).

Wilson, E. O. and Regnier, F. E. (1971) 'The evolution of the alarm defense system in Formicine ants', *American Naturalist*, 105 (943) 279–89.

Wilson, E. O. (1992) *The Diversity of Life*, (Cambridge, Massachusetts: Harvard University Press.)

Wilson, E. O. (1975) *Sociobiology: The New Synthesis* (Cambridge, Mass.: Belknap Press of Harvard University).

Wilz, K. J. (1970) 'Causal and functional analysis of dorsal pricking and nest activity in the courtship of the three spined stickleback (*Agasterosteus aculeatus*)', *Animal Behaviour*, 18, 115–24.

Winn, P., Tarbuck, A. and Dunnett, S. (1984) 'Ibotenic acid lesions of the lateral hypothalamus: comparison with electrolytic lesion syndrome', *Neuroscience*, 12, 225–40.

Wirtshafter, D. and Davis, J. D. (1977) 'Set points, settling points and the control of body weight', *Physiology and Behaviour*, 19, 75–8.

Wolpe, J. (1958) *Psychotherapy for Reciprocal Inhibition* (Stanford, Calif.: Stanford University Press).

Index

203

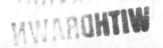